REVIEWS AND TESTIMO...

"Mr. Bromell is a philanthropist in the Conyers/Rockdale communities. In riveting detail, Mr. Bromell powerfully conveys how his faith and work ethic intersected with professional challenges. It is ultimately a testament to his faith, perseverance, and vision. These traits converge to produce a model for entrepreneurial success. His book is an inspirational narrative for anyone pursuing a successful business venture."

—Pamela J. Brown, Chair, Rockdale County Board of Education
Georgia School Board Association District 4 Director

"In his captivating book, Steve reveals how his business expedition unveiled itself as an extraordinary journey of self-discovery. Through unique personal experiences, compelling narratives, relatable themes, and emotional depth, he has expertly employed vivid and life-changing storytelling. The "Grass Clip" sections of the book are certainly not disposable but hold great wisdom for life application for everyone, particularly budding entrepreneurs."

—Kim Dula, PhD, Professor of Leadership and
—Melinda Dula, LLM, Administrative Law Judge

"When most people think of Steve Bromell, they envision an encourager—someone who makes you believe anything is possible. This book proves them all right. Steve's business life has been an incredible journey, and I'm glad I got to take it with him!"

—Shawn Bromell

"You can't make this stuff up! Leave it to Steve Bromell to transparently share his story, his faith, and his legacy. It's apparent that

God trusts Steve with both little and much. Grab this book, pull up a chair, and get ready to be encouraged beyond imagination."

—Miriam Harris Lewis

"Steve Bromell is a man of contagious, life-giving faith that is foundational to his success and significance in business and life. Full of practical wisdom, this book is like a highly effective, inspirational 'boost-shot' of adrenaline that rekindles the courage, perseverance, and faith needed to overcome any obstacle on the way to ultimate victory."

—Fern Taylor, Specialist, Contact Center Technologies and AI

"Steve's depth of faith was forged in uncertain times. His character and business success are testaments to his confidence in Christ. His quiet and consistent faith does all of the talking."

—Craig Johnson

"If there is anyone qualified to write about the intersection of strong faith and professional success, it is Steven Bromell. A man who has mastered the ability to walk among the affluent while leading with deep humility, Steve has penned his business journey in a way that will make you marvel at and want to model his confidence in God, his commitment to excellence in business operations, and his consistent and unwavering perseverance. Whether you are an entrepreneur or serving in another person's enterprise, you can expect to be challenged and encouraged throughout the pages of the book."

—Dr. D'Ann V. Johnson, Founder & CEO
Overflow Ministries Intl.

"Steve Bromell is such an inspiration! How many highly prosperous business owners allow God to pave the way to their success? Humble, giving, and always a beacon of God's glory. What a better place the business world would be if every entrepreneur never lost sight of who is really in charge!"

—Darlene Hotchkiss

If ever I doubted the power of prayer and relying on God, the journey Steven Bromell, took through valleys, hills, and subsequently the mountaintop surely confirms faith beats fear everytime. *Blood, Sweat, and Grass* is a "must read" for any prospective entrepreneur.

—James Oliver Homer, Retired, FedEx Sales

Steven Bromell is a Christ-loving Brother who, being led by the Holy Spirit, shares his testimony journey navigated by the Lord's hand and fueled by Steven's obedience to His Word! Recording real-life stories of recognizing God-size opportunities followed first praising the Lord then stewarding experiences to form God honoring plans is inspiring. Also acknowledging when tragedy and adversity arise, there is a choice to yield to the circumstances or confront them with prayer. Steven relates vividly, making the latter choice often opens a door to witnessing God's miraculous power in real-time action!

—Jeff Beech
"Be a Bridge"... to Restoration
Renew Hope. Strengthen Lives. Bear Fruit.
John 15

BLOOD, SWEAT, AND GRASS

NEVER QUIT ON YOUR DREAMS

M. STEVEN BROMELL

BLOOD, SWEAT, AND GRASS
Never Quit on Your Dreams

Printed in the United States of America
Paperback: 979-8-3363445-3-0
Hardcover: 979-8-9860428-7-9
Hardback Jacket Case Laminate: 979-8-9860428-8-6

Interior and Cover design by: Kingdom Promise Publishing
Published by Kingdom Promise Publishing LLC, Conyers, Georgia
Social Media Handle: @kppublishingllc
KingdomPromisePublishing.com

DEDICATION

The entrepreneurial journey comprises numerous steps where one is either ascending with the hope of success or descending with tears and regrets of failure. To my wife and business partner, Shawn A. Bromell, thank you for believing in me and making the upward journey to success filled with joy and failures met by your love and unwavering support. I dedicate this book to my wife, Shawn, our three amazing sons, Michael Jr., Justin, Chayce, and my Pops, James Oliver Homer.

TABLE OF CONTENTS

ACKNOWLEDGMENTS

To the Kingdom Promise Publishing Team and Marie-Laure Latimore, I want to thank you all for your exceptional work and attention to detail in bringing this book to life. I am forever grateful to all the former and current team members who trusted in my business vision. Thanks to all my family in Little River, South Carolina; Norwalk, Connecticut; Raleigh, North Carolina; Conway, South Carolina; and Conyers, Georgia. I have always been inspired by our upbringing and wanted to represent those who paved the way for us to have a future.

A special thanks to E.M. and H.N. for having my back through some truly rough times. Finally, I want to thank our Pro Cutters team, The Man K.A.V.E., New Covenant Christian Ministry, Lawn Management Network, and the countless people who have inspired and sown valuable seeds throughout my life.

FOREWORD

It is with great pleasure and immense admiration that I introduce this book, penned by a truly extraordinary individual—someone I have been fortunate enough to know for several years. In a world often characterized by uncertainty and challenges, Steve Bromell has faced adversity head-on and has emerged as a beacon of inspiration for all privileged to cross his path.

This book is a testament to the unwavering spirit of a person whose courage knows no bounds. In the face of challenge, Steve has stood firm and encouraged others to find strength within themselves. He will influence you to chase the big dream in your heart through his no-limits mindset. His ability to inspire and uplift those around him is remarkable.

Generosity flows through the very veins of Steve Bromell. Whether it's time, resources, or heartfelt advice, he gives freely and selflessly, embodying the true essence of generosity. His actions speak volumes, reminding us of the profound impact one can have when motivated by a genuine desire to make the world a better place for others and make others better for the world.

Integrity and character are the cornerstones of Steve's being. He remains a steadfast model of virtue in a world where values are sometimes compromised. With the myriad ways to take shortcuts in creating a successful business, it is refreshing to encounter someone willing to go through the process of becoming a successful person. His actions align with his principles, and his words are from a heart of sincerity. It is a rare privilege to witness someone living with such authenticity, and through these pages, you will undoubtedly catch a glimpse of the moral fortitude that guides his every step.

Perhaps most inspiring is his unwavering belief in living according to scripture. In a world that often veers from spiritual guidance, Steve remains rooted in his faith, drawing strength and wisdom from the timeless teachings that have guided generations. His faith is exemplified in his professional life as well as his personal life. His life is a testament to the transformative power of living with purpose, guided by principles that transcend the short-lived nature of the world.

As you embark on the journey through these pages, I encourage you to open your heart and mind to the profound insights and wisdom he shares. This book will be a source of inspiration, a call to courage, a reminder of the boundless impact one person can have, and a testament to the enduring power of a life lived with integrity, generosity, and unwavering faith.

With deep respect and admiration,
Billy R. Johnson
Senior Pastor, New Covenant Christian Ministries

INTRODUCTION

I found a hub of success and opportunities in the vibrant city of "Hotlanta," better known as Atlanta, Georgia. When I relocated to the city in late 1992, I had no idea it would ignite my dormant entrepreneurial spirit. I was born in Norwalk, Connecticut, and shuttled between my birthplace and South Carolina during my early years. After attending North Myrtle Beach High School and serving in the United States Army, my dream of entrepreneurship finally blossomed in Atlanta.

Working diligently for Federal Express *(known as FedEx)* and fulfilling my monthly duties as a Georgia National Guardsman, I felt an incessant itch that remained unsatisfied until I took a leap of faith into business ownership. While I wish I could boast immediate success after the leap, as my godfather "Pops" often reminded me, life is about facing reality. He would say, "That's a good Easter speech, Steven, now tell me what's real!"

Whether you're at the beginning of your journey, contemplating a new career launch, or well into the pursuit of your dreams, this book is guaranteed to inject a powerful dose of adrenaline into your aspirations. There were numerous occasions when I found myself sitting, shaking my head, on the brink of conceding to yet another failure. Yet, in those moments, a glimmer of hope would emerge urging me to invest a bit more time, exert a little more effort, find the silver lining, believe in myself, and declare, "If not me, then who?"

Frequently, this hope arrived in the form of an inspirational book, revitalizing my spirit, and reinforcing the notion that failures are nothing more than stepping-stones on the path to ultimate success. Perhaps you, like me, have experienced the sting of hurtful comments and felt discouraged—convinced that no one takes you seriously. Don't allow quitting or never starting to be the final script of your life for you are so much more. In this book, you'll discover that the magnitude of the obstacle should fuel an even stronger response. Overcoming challenges is immensely rewarding.

Even as I grappled with doubts about whether my story was worthy of being put into print, I realized that not writing it would unequivocally answer that question in the negative. The essence of the American dream lies in seizing the time we are given and maximizing its potential. If you've ever doubted whether growth and success are attainable—whether due to your upbringing, the side of the tracks you live on, an absence of inheritance, life's ups and downs, tragedies, insufficient funding, faded accomplishments of your youth, or simply challenging circumstances—think again. This book will demonstrate that anything is possible for those willing to exert a triumphant effort.

Perhaps you find yourself feeling stuck, sensing there's more for you to accomplish. Or, like me, you believed you had done enough, only to realize that the chapters of your life are still being written. You've chosen the right book! While there are no guarantees in life, one thing is certain—if you quit, that is a guarantee of not achieving your goals. So, lace up your boots, dust off your book of dreams, recognize that you're already at the starting line, and let's go for it!

In this book, you will embark on the genuine journey of a defiant country boy who ventured into the world guided by books and life lessons. Eventually, he found his path to the gateway of the south. Despite numerous setbacks, a series of failures, deferred hope, closed doors, and countless rejections— all accompanied by a chorus of "you cannot," "you are not qualified," and flat-out being told "no" time and time again—he pressed on. Grab a comfy blanket, settle into a nice chair, and immerse yourself in this triumphant story of remarkable resilience, perseverance, and unwavering determination. Prepare to read, cry, laugh, and savor the inspiring tale of overcoming unbelievable setbacks.

Chapter One

IN THE BEGINNING

*I*n 1979, Hurricane David slammed into Myrtle Beach, South Carolina, shaking up my second hometown of Little River. Our living situation was humble—a single-wide trailer lacking running water and with sporadic electricity. Our restroom was a brief stroll away, next to my dear aunt's house along a dirt path. Despite the typical hurricane warnings advising us to seek sturdier shelter, we had no means of transportation, so we'd bunker down and hope for the best sending our prayers skyward.

During such unpredictable events, the mind becomes a whirlwind of thoughts. Mentally, I'd wander to unfamiliar places envisioning myself running, laughing, and enjoying care-free moments. I'd imagine the simple joys of strolling through the neighborhood shooting hoops until exhaustion set in. But reality swiftly intruded with the wind's howl and the trailer's relentless rocking reminding me of the storm's presence.

Eventually, my siblings and I would drift off to sleep, often huddled close together, only to awaken to the tranquility of daylight. It seemed as if the storm never occurred until we dared to step outside. And then, the truth became clear. Nature's fury had left its mark. As the designated bathroom pioneer, I braved the path first.

Approaching closer, I found nothing but shattered wood and a gaping void where our outhouse once stood. Standing amidst the wreckage, I scanned the surroundings, half-expecting to spot another outhouse nearby. But I soon realized my mistake—and as if to emphasize it, I heard voices growing louder, morphing into laughter as others gathered around the demolished structure.

Certain moments etch themselves into the fabric of our lives, and this was undoubtedly one of them. With tears welling in my eyes, I peered into the void only to find it teeming with maggots writhing amidst the wreckage. In that poignant moment, it struck me that even the humblest of beings possess the innate ability to transcend their circumstances—to continue to live beyond their humble origins. It was a revelation that ignited a resolve within me, a determination to rise above poverty, scorn, and derision, refusing to be defined by the laughter and condescension of others.

An Unexpected Move

"Steven, can we talk?" The voice belonged to the man I revered as my godfather, a figure who had assumed a paternal role in my life, a bond that would endure through the years. We resided in Stone Mountain, Georgia, and both were employed at Federal Express—he worked in corporate sales, and I worked as a part-time box sorter and driver. His request didn't trigger any alarm bells; our relationship was built on openness and trust. While his recollection of the conversation might differ, this is how I recall it. "I'm relocating to Southwest Atlanta," he disclosed, referring to it as "The SWATS," a nickname we often used.

My mind raced as I processed the news. The city is thirty to forty-five minutes away from everything I'd grown accustomed to in metro Atlanta. "When are we moving and what's the new neighborhood like?" I fired off questions, but he abruptly cut me off. "I'm moving, but you'll have to find somewhere else to live." His words hit me like an unexpected gut punch leaving me reeling. With a heavy heart, I could only muster a solemn, "okay," in response.

The Start of Something New

One Sunday, my Pops invited me to lunch at a new restaurant called "This is It." As we drove there, I kept asking him for details about the restaurant and its location. We shared some hearty laughs along the way, and he explained to me what kind of restaurant it was. Of course, I was eager for some down-home barbecue. The parking lot was busy, but after some searching, we finally found a spot.

As we got out of the car, my ears suddenly began to ring. Amidst the bustling sounds of the surroundings, I distinctly heard my full name being called out. Everyone typically referred to me by my proper name, Steven Bromell, so I searched for the source of the familiar voice. Across from the restaurant, I noticed an apartment complex, and my eyes caught sight of someone crossing four lanes of busy traffic. To my surprise, it was none other than my future roommate and business partner —a friend from Longs, South Carolina. I had no idea he had moved to Atlanta. The last I had heard; he had joined the military after high school.

I'm sure my Pops thought we were crazy as we practically knocked each other to the ground and embraced like long-lost brothers! It was clear that God always had a plan. He joined us for lunch, and we caught up on each other's lives since the last time we had seen each other, which was while partying on the beach. Everything changed from there.

About a year and a few months later in our living room, my new roommate, affectionately dubbed Room Dog, or RD, among other nicknames, and I engaged in a casual chat about our aspirations. I confessed my long-standing desire to delve into the world of business, yet I remained uncertain about the specifics such as what type of business to pursue or how to make it all work.

His jaw practically hit the floor—he harbored the same aspirations. As our conversation unfolded, he shared about his maternal grandfather, also known as Granddaddy. This patriarch owned extensive land and engaged in farming back in our hometown, which we fondly referred to as The Beach. All the small towns were within a 20- to 25-minute radius of each other, hence the nickname. Room Dog gleaned a robust work ethic from his years toiling on the farm under his grandfather's tutelage. Over time, he regaled me with tales of his grandfather's ownership of numerous beachfront properties that he was forced to redeem for properties several miles away from the highly sought after beachfront.

After our initial conversation, RD informed me that he had two cousins who were also keen on venturing into business. I happened to know them both. We agreed that the next step would be for all of us to meet and discuss things further. We scheduled a date and time then convened at our apartment in Lithonia, Georgia. Over the next six months, we bonded, sharing laughter, jokes, and memories. We exchanged stories and ideas stemming from our hometowns, mutual acquaintances, and a plethora of business concepts.

Time for Action

We lacked money, resources, and business acumen. Despite the obvious, at the six-month mark, someone blurted out, "How about we start cutting grass?" We exchanged glances and then simultaneously exclaimed, "Yeah, let's do it!" That very day, we quickly assigned roles. My mind raced as I tried to work out the logistics. The following day, I headed to the library to research lawn care and gather statistics for our new business venture. Over the next several meetings, we brainstormed on how to get started, but there was one small problem: none of us had any money, and I knew my credit was a mess!

After extensive discussion, with my sole credit card—a Target card with a $200 limit—I offered to make the purchase. Knowing little about lawn care, I reasoned that our priority was to acquire a lawn mower. I headed to Target and bought our inaugural mower along with a push broom, shovel, and handheld hedge clippers that resembled oversized scissors. As the cashier totaled up the items, the cost hovered just under my $200 charge limit.

Grass Clips

When starting a business, one often envisions widespread interest, eager support, and perhaps even investment from others. Unfortunately, in many cases, this optimistic outlook proves to be nothing more than a pipe dream.

We convened a meeting to decide on a name for our business, which was essential for obtaining the necessary business license. After tossing around several ideas, we settled on something that would pay homage to the towns we hailed from. I originated from Little River, South Carolina; while RD and his cousins hailed from Longs, South Carolina. Eventually, we agreed upon "Double 'L' Lawn Care," representing both Longs and Little River. We made a pact to never disclose the meaning behind the name. That decision turned out to be a brilliant marketing tactic. We played up the secrecy surrounding the name keeping people guessing and intrigued. Many assumed it had something to do with our last names ending with two Ls, a clever but incorrect assumption. Since our small towns weren't widely recognized, when people asked where we were from, we simply said "Myrtle Beach," a name more familiar to most.

Who Needs Their Grass Cut?

Turning to my godfather, a steadfast supporter and encourager of all my endeavors, I sought his help in creating a flyer. Together, we crafted a simple design with a catchy tagline: "If your grass is not becoming of you, you should be coming to us. Let us cut your grass. Double 'L' Lawn Care." Fueled by excitement, I was convinced that everyone with a home would be eager to enlist our services. We distributed countless flyers, but to our disappointment, we only received one response—from my trusted Pops. He graciously responded, "If you don't mind coming to Southwest Atlanta, you can cut my grass."

Clad in our ex-military Battle Dress Uniform, also known as BDUs, with camouflage pants and brown T-shirts, RD and I armed ourselves with the brand-new lawnmower. We hopped into my green Ford Ranger, while his cousins followed in their vehicle. Despite our enthusiasm, our preparation fell short. Upon reaching our first lawn, we hastily exited our vehicles only to realize that our lawnmower was still in its box and needed assembling.

The neighborhood, old with many trees and old-style high curbing, had a medium-sized lawn and overgrown hedges wrapped around the house, left me feeling a bit dizzy. As we all grabbed tools, we set to work. RD and his cousins started edging the lawn with a shovel, clearing debris, and trimming the hedges, while I assembled the mower. Two hours later, we were ready to mow. With a few pulls, the engine roared to life, and we tackled our first lawn. Despite our lack of experience, our determination compensated for it.

After approximately four- to five-long hours, we finished; and quite honestly, it was not the most professional job ever done, to say the least. I went to knock on Pop's door to thank him for letting us do his lawn and tell him it was free. He immediately stopped me mid-sentence and told me that he understood we were just starting and not to feel obligated to do him or anyone else favors because business is business.

We were unsure what to charge him, so he pulled out three twenty-dollar bills and paid us sixty dollars for cutting his lawn. Exhausted and uncertain about what we had gotten ourselves into, we held a quick meeting at the tailgate as we packed all our equipment in the truck. We discussed what to do with our earnings. As I may not have mentioned before, we were all Christian men, so we believed we should give it back to a church as a seed offering. Though it was a novel idea and went against the norm, we all agreed to this course of action and set out to decide which church would be the beneficiary.

We decided to stay in the neighborhood and find something local. As we drove along, like an epiphany, the light shone directly on a church. The light was golden and crispy—it was Church's Chicken. We went inside and devoured a bucket of chicken, honey biscuits, and sweet tea with our hard-earned money! The leftover cash went into our gas tanks, and the business dream was off and running.

With our first customer secured, we encountered the classic dilemma that most entrepreneurs face and asked ourselves, OK, genius businessperson, what's next? We returned to our apartment with full bellies, a tank of gas, and a lawnmower in the back of my truck. Despite exhaustion and the looming five a.m. start for my regular job at Federal Express, excitement coursed through me as I pondered the possibilities for the weeks and months ahead. Pulling up to our apartment complex, we unloaded the mower and lugged it up three stories to our patio, which happened to be through my room. This routine would become our norm for many months to come.

The Silent Auction

Through one of the guys, we learned about a unique opportunity to donate a service through a silent auction. Unfortunately, I was unable to attend the event, but the rest of the guys got decked out in black tie. I must say they represented well. At the time, we had very little idea what we were doing, but we knew we were hard workers and would figure it out. We ended up donating our services to a very popular anchor for one of the local news stations that lived in a prominent neighborhood. Additionally, we had the opportunity to meet a community organizer in the county where we lived that would prove to be very helpful down the road.

While we were waiting to set up the "free service," my Pops came through again, and we secured our second customer who was a good friend of his. I'll never forget working extremely hard, edging her entire lawn with a shovel, and sweeping up the debris with a push broom. Reflecting on that moment today, all I can say is "God, you have brought us a very long way!"

Why Atlanta?

At the age of 17, I had this crazy idea of moving to Maryland and starting a business. I had no connections to the state, nor did I know what kind of business I wanted to start. I had my best friend and another high school friend, and we were determined to move, start a business, and figure it out as we went along.

As fate would have it, one day while I was working in a bowling alley, one of my big brother's good friends, who was serving in the US Marines, walked in wearing his Army uniform. I have no idea why he was there; perhaps he wanted to bowl I reasoned. Suddenly, he approached me as if he was on a mission from on high. The Army Sergeant said, "Little B, as most of my brothers' friends referred to me, what are you going to do after high school?" I looked at him, and I know this is going to sound unbelievable, but without any pause, much thought, consideration, or anything else, I responded, "I am going to join the Army." Just like that, my life course changed.

I originally envisioned myself heading to college on a cross-country scholarship if the business idea did not pan out, but severe shin splints thwarted that plan, causing me to doubt my abilities. Joining the military appeared to offer the next best opportunity to escape Little River, South Carolina. To carve out my path, I enlisted on the spot. I even requested the recruiter to send me as far away from the Myrtle Beach area as possible. I should have been careful with what I wished for! Honestly, thoughts of venturing into business were far from my mind during my army service. I simply lived in the moment, embracing as much fun as possible while serving.

After serving five years in the US Army, I found myself unsure of my next steps. Frankly, the skills I had acquired in the Army did not seem to translate well to what we call "the real world." In the military, I worked as a petroleum fuel specialist, essentially a "gas man." While the role was more detailed than that, I had no idea how to apply it outside of the military. By this time, my Pops had relocated to Atlanta from Connecticut, and I had visited him a few times while stationed at my last duty station in Ft. Polk, Louisiana. I had no desire to move back to Little River, and the idea of relocating to Maryland or Connecticut seemed like a possibility, but also a stretch, to say the least.

Shortly after my stint in the Army concluded, I received a phone call from my Pops that altered the course of my life. He said, "Son, you can move to Atlanta with me, free of room and board." The sheer generosity of his offer made me feel like I could leap over the moon. I wasted no time eagerly making my way there. When people inquire about my decision to choose Atlanta, the answer is straightforward: I didn't have many viable or realistic options at the time. Plus, during a weekend visit, I stumbled upon a club called The Sandcastle and was instantly captivated. And let's not forget about the free rent. Who in their right mind would pass up such an opportunity?!

Fast Forward: The Silent Auction

The customer finally scheduled the donated service, something we hadn't tackled before: cleaning gutters. The two of us tackled this job together, and I'll admit, I was relieved when my partner insisted on climbing onto the roof to handle the gutters. Somehow, we managed to complete the task. Like all our early work, it felt like it took forever to finish. I hoped this job would open the floodgates for us, but unfortunately, it seemed like we hit a brick wall. We rode through neighborhoods dropping off flyers, anxiously waiting for the phone to ring, and checking messages for callbacks. Most of the responses turned out to be people just looking for estimates, not actual hires. Shortly after, two of our guys decided the venture was not for them and graciously backed out of Double "L" Lawn Care leaving myself and my roommate RD to continue.

The Power of Persistence

Nonetheless, I was determined—fueled by courage—to just go for it! There was an enormous subdivision around the corner from where we lived, so I packed the lawnmower into the green Ford Ranger and set off. With extreme nervousness, but confidence from within, I parked the truck in front of a lawn that needed mowing. Armed with the cheapest flyers you ever saw, I knocked on the door and then took a few steps back, ensuring I would not be too close when the homeowner opened it.

When the first person opened the door and asked if she could help me, I greeted her with a polite "good afternoon, Ma'am," and introduced myself as Steve. I explained that I had a mower in the back of the truck and had just started a lawn care business. I inquired if she needed her lawn cut. Despite her polite refusal, I wasn't going to be deterred by one "no".

Grass Clips

If you are looking to start a business or
do anything worthwhile, put a comma behind
every NO and keep moving towards
the Next Opportunity.

I thanked the homeowner for her time, but instead of moving on to the next house, I decided to try another street. After approaching about three houses, a door opened, and I delivered the same pitch as before. I greeted her with "Good afternoon, Ma'am," and introduced myself as Steve. I explained that I had a mower in the back of the truck and had just started a lawn care business, asking if she needed her lawn cut. This time, the lady responded by asking me to tell her more. Caught off guard, I admitted, "Well, I have no idea what I'm doing or how much to charge you, but I am a hard worker. If you're satisfied with my work, pay me what you think I deserve; if not, don't pay me a thing." Looking back, I wonder if I had been drinking or smoking something to use that pitch! Surprisingly, it worked, and I stuck with that sales approach. Remarkably, no one ever stiffed me, and we began building our client base from there. Despite our efforts, progress was slow, and we were not gaining the momentum we had hoped for. In every startup journey, there comes a moment, or perhaps many, where you must take a long, deep pause and ask yourself, Is this really worth the hassle? Fortunately, shortly after those contemplations, our church leaders announced they were hosting a business expo. My mind began to churn as Room Dog and I strategized how we could represent ourselves and build our clientele list at the event.

Once again, I could not attend this opportunity due to my work schedule, but thankfully, RD could. We prepared a marketing visual with grass and various mulches, along with flyers and business cards. We were off and running hoping to grow by leaps and bounds. The expo turned out to be a success for us. RD's magnetic personality helped us make some great contacts, and we received numerous requests for estimates.

Grass Clips

Whenever things seem dark, seek the light.
Remember who called you and why you have been called.
Dreams Require Action.

This single opportunity catapulted us into growth. At the time, we considered anything with more than five customers as extreme growth! Starting a lawn care company was not something I had ever considered. I would have had choice words for anyone who suggested such a thing for me to do. Instead, I had envisioned myself with a briefcase, striding confidently into a high-rise, and representing business in a polished environment. As an exercise of my faith, I would put on the only suit I had at the time and headed to Lenox Square Mall in Atlanta. Once there, with my boxed briefcase in tow, I strolled around a bit before settling in the food court. I opened my briefcase, pretending to read papers or books, trying to exude an air of importance. I wanted to experience what it felt like to have made it.

I know it sounds a little crazy, but whenever I start to feel complacent, I recall those hopeful days! Someone once told me that I was doing the "fake it until you make it" dance. At first, I brushed it off, thinking, "Yeah, that's one way to put it." Yet, I genuinely believed I was envisioning my future during those moments.

With the support of our church family and word-of-mouth spreading, we managed to purchase our first trailer. Despite this progress, we still had to remove the mower from the truck daily and haul it up three flights of stairs, through my bedroom, and onto the balcony. After several weeks with the trailer, we received notice from our apartment complex leasing agent: we could not store a trailer on the premises, and we had just 48 hours to remove it.

Sometimes, God allows adversities to come our way to propel us to greater heights. In response to the notice from our apartment complex, we searched the local area and found a storage facility. We leased a five-by-ten area, which suited our needs perfectly, given the small size of our trailer. Unexpectedly, there was a challenge: the storage bay was sloped. This meant that every night, we had to unhook the trailer from my Ford Ranger and push it into the storage bay.

During this time, my four-year-old son, Michael, Jr., came to live with my roommate and me. I set up a small bed in my room for him and enrolled him in the school at our church. Each day, I would drop him off early in the morning, head to my regular job, and pick him up when I finished. Back at the apartment, I'd make sure he had something to eat before loading up the equipment and heading out to mow lawns, with him in tow. Since many of our customers were church members, they graciously watched him for me while we worked on their lawns. I understand that this arrangement wasn't ideal, but in the late nineties, it was a different time. We usually finished around 8 to 9:30 p.m., dropped off the trailer, and repeated the routine the next day.

A Peek into the Past: Tobacco Harvesting

In Little River, South Carolina, one of the primary sources of income was tobacco harvesting. Everyone in the community was expected to participate. Coming from Norwalk, Connecticut; this way of life was somewhat foreign to me as it differed from my birthplace. We were instilled with the value of hard work, regardless of the task at hand, even if it wasn't something we enjoyed. Hunger and poverty were indifferent to how they were satisfied.

I was deemed too small to work in the fields at the ripe age of 11 years old, so I was assigned the task of "laying sticks." This job paid fifteen dollars per day and involved waiting for the barn ladies to place tobacco leaves on a conveyor belt with the stems facing toward me. My role was to lay a stick across the leaves. Once I did, they would add a second layer on top. After that, the stringer would bind the stems together. This allowed the hanger assistant to pick up the bundle and hand it to the person who would hang the tobacco inside the barn. I found this process fascinating, especially since they would often be hanging upside down when receiving the sticks.

Not to mention the remarkable precision with which the field guys would "crop that tobacco" and lay it on the trailer, driven by the coolest guy on the team—the tractor driver. During our short lunch break, we would be provided with a soda and a nab *(Nabisco crackers)*. If you were prepared, you might have brought sardines, tuna fish, or Vienna sausages with crackers.

Through this experience, I learned the value of hard work, and humility, and gained clarity on what I did not want to do with my life if I had any say in the matter.

A New Partnership

My phone rang, and it was RD. I answered to hear him say, "I got a call from the church leaders. They want us to cut their property." Initially, I was overjoyed at the prospect, until the sheer size of the property dawned on me. With our limited resources—a single 21-inch residential style lawn mower—I felt a pang of doubt. Determined not to be defeated, we agreed to take on the challenge and figure it out later. RD scheduled the work for the next day, and I worked hard at Federal Express to finish early. There was an immense sense of excitement for this significant opportunity.

Arriving at the site, grass towering over our heads greeted us. At that moment, I questioned my decision. Yet, it was too late to turn back. We plunged into the task, and despite the odds, we managed to complete the property. Surprisingly, our work turned out rather well, considering we only had one mower. The head maintenance person was pleased and offered us our very first commercial contract. The elation we felt was akin to winning the lottery! With this contract in hand, we wasted no time. We promptly purchased another mower and began investing in gas-powered equipment such as a blower, weed trimmer, and edger. All our purchases were made at Home Depot, as we were unaware of specialized commercial landscape equipment dealers.

Shortly after securing our first commercial account for Double "L" Lawn Care, RD approached me with a significant decision: he was ready to leave his regular job and commit to the lawn care business full-time. I was thrilled by this news, as it demonstrated a level of commitment that I knew would be essential for our success. RD gave his two weeks' notice and immediately began seeking new business opportunities. In those early days, I would join him at worksites after finishing my shift at Federal Express. At the time I felt torn about getting rid of my security net working at Federal Express.

An Invitation to Change—Looking Back

Every Sunday morning, I engaged in a spirited game of basketball with the guys from Federal Express. We frequented a couple of downtown gyms, and the matches were always intense and served as a great source of recreation. During the early years of living in metro Atlanta, attending church had not even crossed my mind. My priorities revolved around three things: taking care of my son, working, and enjoying the party scene as if it were going out of style.

Crossroads often emerge when you've exhausted the possibilities along one path marking a split in the road. Yet, there are moments when you find yourself at a crossroads and don't realize it until much later. At a crossroads, your decisions can either alter your destiny or fulfill it. One such moment came when my Pops knocked on my bedroom door as I was preparing to head out to play ball, asking, "Steven, why don't you come to church with me today?" Normally, he took my son to church while I pursued my interests and then we would meet up later for lunch or dinner.

This specific time, something in his voice suggested he was not in the mood for a refusal, so I agreed. Hastily throwing on clothes and grabbing the baby bag, we set off to the church, about 25 minutes away with its small congregation. The pastor proved to be intense, funny, charismatic, and an excellent speaker. Sensing the need for an easy exit, I positioned myself at the very back of the church, ready to slip away unnoticed if necessary.

Then, during the sermon, the pastor abruptly halted his preaching and called out, "Excuse me, sir." Bewildered, I glanced around, wondering whom he was addressing. After he repeated himself several times, it became evident that he was speaking to me, especially when he added, "Yes, you with the baby." Feeling a surge of suppressed anger in my chest, I reluctantly acknowledged him with a "Yes." He instructed me to come to the front row and take a seat. Reluctantly, I complied. Strangely, he did not say anything else to me that day. Even more peculiar, I never played basketball on a Sunday again after that encounter.

A Leap of Faith

Six months after RD quit his job, I found myself still delivering packages. One day, while descending the steps to make a delivery, a sudden vision flashed before my eyes: it was twenty years into the future, and I was still on the same route. The realization that I hadn't progressed in life startled me. At that moment, I decided to end my time at Federal Express. I submitted my two weeks' notice the next day, for my destiny beckoned me forward.

Seeking support, I talked to my mother and other family members. To my surprise, the encouragement I expected was lacking. Many questioned why I would leave a stable job to work outdoors in the hot sun cutting grass. I was warned about the financial risks of having a partner and cautioned that such arrangements often do not end well. Despite the doubts from others, I remained steadfast in my decision to pursue a new path.

As the years passed, I came to realize that much of the apprehension surrounding my decision stemmed from a common fear of the unknown and a tendency to cling to familiarity. Despite feeling determined, excited, and scared all at once, I remained steadfast in my resolve. The two weeks flew by quickly, and I punched out for the last time at Federal Express. I left on good terms, having been an easy employee to manage. Throughout my tenure, I approached my work with precision, thoroughness, speed, and honesty. I held firm to the belief that regardless of the job or its compensation, giving my best effort was non-negotiable.

During my first week as a full-time business owner, I decided to sleep in until the phone woke me up. After all, isn't that what bosses do? The caller was a telemarketer trying to sell me on a multi-level marketing scheme. With unwavering confidence, I informed him that I already had a business and preferred to invest my resources into building it rather than someone else's venture.

His response caught me off guard; it was unexpected and confrontational. He questioned why I was still at home in bed at that hour if I was serious about my business. His words struck a nerve, and I felt a surge of anger. After exchanging some heated words with him, I hung up the phone. As I sat on the edge of the bed, reflecting on the encounter, I could not shake the realization that he was right. Why was I still at home when I should have been out working? During my time at Federal Express, I had grown accustomed to waking up early every day, yet here I was allowing myself a moment of relaxation.

At that moment, I realized I had to confront my fears of cold calling and hit the pavement to ensure the success of the business, which needed to support two young men and a child. I rose from the bed, got dressed in khakis and a button-up shirt, and began knocking on the doors of numerous businesses that day—introducing them to our grass-cutting services. With each presentation, my confidence grew, and my pitch improved. Despite my efforts, we did not secure a single client from that day's endeavors. I gained something far more valuable: by adhering to the scripture that says, "Faith without works is dead."

I demonstrated my commitment by putting in the effort, regardless of the specific outcome.

Grass Clips

Remaining attuned to the Spirit of God is essential.
While you may not always comprehend how
He is orchestrating events on your behalf,
you can find solace in knowing that
He is indeed at work.

The following day, I heard a knock on our apartment door. Upon answering, I found the maintenance guy from our apartment complex standing there. He inquired, "Don't you guys have a lawn care company?" With pride, I confirmed, "Yes, we do!" He then informed me, "Well, I wanted to give you a heads-up that we are looking for a new service provider." Expressing gratitude for the information, I asked him for the contact details of the person making the hiring decision. He provided me with the necessary information before departing.

Feeling uncertain about the next steps, I decided to have a conversation with RD. We concluded that we would draft a proposal to present to the apartment complex. With the help of a friend who lent me her typewriter, I wrote up a proposal outlining our lawn care services. Despite my lack of experience in this area, I believed that by keeping the proposal simple and demonstrating our capability to perform the work, I could manage the task at hand.

For the next few days, I dedicated myself to refining the proposal and making corrections and adjustments until it was just right. With our proposal finalized, the next step was the presentation. We agreed that I would be the one to present the information to the leasing manager. Donning my winning suit—the same one I used to wear to the mall with my briefcase —I felt confident as I walked into the meeting. And just as we had hoped, we closed the deal! We secured our second commercial account. This was a tremendous relief as it meant we could now pay our rent on time.

Grass Clips

Trust in God, exercise patience, and maintain a consistent work ethic. Then, when opportunity knocks, you will not need to scramble to prepare—you'll already be fully equipped to seize the moment.

In the times ahead, our church experienced rapid growth, after quickly outgrowing our space in Decatur, Georgia. Recognizing this, the leadership decided to relocate to a larger church location in Stone Mountain, Georgia. This move, which brought us closer to our apartment, proved to be a pivotal moment in our journey.

After securing our second commercial account, we encountered a small issue: we had but two small mowers and two employees, RD and myself. Believing in the power of hard work, we tackled the main part of the apartment complex, dedicating an entire day to the task. The following day, we addressed the second part, and despite the challenge, we managed to complete all the work.

As we continued to work on existing accounts and attract new clients, we realized the importance of strategy. We implemented a plan where we dedicated each day to specific areas allowing us to maximize our time and serve a larger number of clients efficiently. Before this strategy, we wasted time driving all over metro Atlanta for just a couple of lawns that were spread out over long distances. Our change in approach made a significant difference.

Chapter Two

A CALL OF DISAPPOINTMENT

Push Past it!

*O*ne day, as we were out cutting the church property, I glanced near our equipment trailer and noticed it was empty. Assuming my business partner moved the equipment to use it, I walked around the other side of the building and saw him diligently working with one piece of equipment. Waving my hands, I approached him, and as he turned off his weed trimmer, he asked if everything was okay. I expressed uncertainty but suggested he could help by telling me where he put our equipment. Bewildered, he replied that he hadn't moved any equipment. Unfortunately, our equipment had been stolen, and to compound the issue, we had not saved up any money to replace it. Naïvely, I assumed the church would assist us, only later realizing it was not their responsibility even though the theft occurred on their property.

Grass Clips

Many people dive into business without the
necessary guidance, tools, administrative skills,
and to their detriment, insurance.
I would not recommend it.

On a mission, we drove around the area and stopped at a few pawn shops close to the property hoping to find the thieves and recover our equipment. Unfortunately, as is often the case with lawn equipment, it was long gone. This incident shook me to my core. Immediately after renting equipment to complete the job, I sought an insurance agent and secured property insurance for the new equipment we would need to purchase. The loss propelled us into high gear, driving us to drum up more business so we could replace what was taken.

From Renting to Owning

During my early years in Norwalk, Connecticut, my family usually rented houses and never owned them. When we moved to South Carolina, we had to live with my grandmother and step-grandfather. After about a year, my mother got us a trailer, albeit without lights and running water. Despite that, I was happy to be in a place that was ours. I yearned for the day when I could live in and own a home.

Through our client list from the church, we met a couple who worked in real estate and were willing to assist us in purchasing a home. RD and I decided to embark on this journey together with the home in my name. The process proved to be challenging with one hurdle after another. During my time serving in the Army, I made several poor financial decisions resulting in late payments that now came back to haunt me. Additionally, while stationed overseas in Korea, I entrusted someone else with the responsibility of making my car payments, which resulted in further late payments.

Despite these challenges, it seemed we were on track to successfully navigate through the process. We looked at several homes and finally settled on one that was under construction with about thirty percent left for completion. We put the home under contract while still trying to secure financing. Having been away from my regular job for many months, the agent asked me if I had any recent check stubs. Unfortunately, I had nothing up to date to provide.

We frequently visited the house to help the contractor with tasks like hanging doors and ceilings. I even brought my mother and sisters along to show them my progress. Additionally, I contacted my former manager at Federal Express to inquire about job opportunities. He was delighted to hear from me, and we began the paperwork for my return. I went to the corporate office and even took a drug test to secure this opportunity and maintain my reputation as a future homeowner. It's remarkable what I was willing to sacrifice just so others perceive me as successful.

I want to clarify that I wasn't pressured into buying a home; it was more about my ego and pride than anything else. I understood that I needed to stay on the job for at least six months to qualify for a loan, so I set everything up at Federal Express. I passed the drug test and completed all the paperwork. To this day, I still remember my employee number, almost as if 169331 was etched in my brain! There is nothing wrong with working a nine-to-five, but I knew it wasn't my calling. Instead, I was acting on my selfish desires.

Finally, my first day back had arrived. I woke up super early that morning and had a profound encounter with the voice of God. He said very clearly, "Son, if you go back to that job, you will never leave it". I sat on the edge of my bed in shock and fear. After gathering my thoughts, I picked up the phone and dialed the station where I would be reporting back to work.

When my manager answered, he greeted me cheerfully, expressing his excitement to have me back. Once I informed him that I would not be coming back that morning or ever, his cheerfulness quickly turned to anger. Then, he cursed at me. Despite his reaction, I apologized, thanked him, and never looked back! Since we were not able to secure the loan, we had to move on. Even with being disappointed, I thanked God for intervening and making me realize that obtaining things apart from His will would cost me much more than a moment of fleeting joy and impressing others.

The Rewards of Trust

Several months later, the real estate couple from the church gave me a call and asked a simple question: "Do you have your bags packed to move?" Confused, I asked the two of them to repeat the statement. They reiterated, and it became clear they had stumbled upon a program that could help us achieve our goal of owning a home. With a down payment of $5,000, which we bartered with a client for, and instructions to pay off several bills using money orders, we were suddenly back in the game. One of my dreams was finally within arm's reach.

We found a home, closed the deal, and encountered an unexpected challenge: we were going to be homeless for about 2 months because our lease was up before we could move into our new home. Yet, for the first time in my life, I would soon live in a home that was not rented or on wheels. As I slept on a couple of friends couches I remembered the sounds of that horn blowing super early in the morning rounding up daily field workers, the laughter by the outhouse, the smirks, and feelings of shame as I paid for penny candy with food stamps, the hand-me-down clothes, and the overall sense of hopelessness all seemed to be a distant past as we prepared to move into our new home.

With a simple flip of a coin, we decided who would get upstairs and who would live in the basement portion of the home. I ended up with the basement, which I believed to be the better area since it had its own living room, exercise room, and laundry room, although I would have been okay upstairs as well. Over the next couple of years, we continued to build the business one customer at a time. We had a small housewarming gathering, and our parents came down to celebrate our success. For the first time I could remember, my mom told me how proud she was of me.

An Unexpected Relationship

As young children, we were always in church for something, whether it was the children's choir rehearsal, Sunday School, or a revival. The church doors were always open. I was so immersed in church activities that I silently vowed to distance myself so far away from it as an adult that I would need to send God a postcard for Him to find me. Now, here I was, supporting multiple ministries, recruiting new members, sharing Christ, and loving it! Unbeknownst to me, my destiny was intertwined with my newly built relationship with Christ and the church I attended.

The sky was bright and clear on this fourth Sunday of the month. It was my turn to serve as part of the parking lot ministry. Our church growth had exploded, and we had to double and triple park cars because of the overflow of members and visitors. Some members of the parking team had a tradition where, upon seeing someone attractive, they would jokingly vie for the chance to park the vehicle first. I know that sounds awful, but remember I was building my relationship with God. He did not send me to save the world!

As she turned her signal on to enter the parking lot, I promise you my heart skipped a beat, and immediately I raised my hand as a signal to the rest of the guys to back off. I was parking her car with VIP treatment. She had the top down on her convertible, and she was simply stunning! I parked her car and said hello as she moved on to the sanctuary for service. We did not speak again for months, but that day was one I will never forget.

During another Sunday service, I heard our Pastor's voice calling out, "Will all the men please stand up and sit on the steps to allow the ladies to sit down?" We had three services, and the last two consistently were standing room only. I loved it when he made that announcement because it gave me a bird's eye view of all the customers I needed to see for collections after service and, oh yeah, the cuties in the crowd as well! There was one young lady that I had my eye on. Like clockwork, she would be fashionably late every Sunday and occupy the front row. She wore red lipstick, and it was the reddest color I had ever seen in my life. We would lock eyes for moments at a time, gazing at each other.

After several months of this, the church continued to grow. We were maxing out the parking lot and parking cars a few blocks away at a local high school. I decided the day had come for me to get her number or give her mine. I was driving the church van and noticed she was in our overflow parking lot, so I timed it to make sure I would have her as a rider. I approached her and asked, "Would you like a lift to your car?" She agreed, bringing her best friend. Off we went. As she was getting out of the van, I stopped her, slipped my number in her hand and asked her to call me later. I was pleasantly surprised when I got home; she called, and I asked her out. Subsequently, I eagerly awaited my date with the young lady I had been admiring for months. She agreed to meet me at my apartment where I planned to drive us on our inaugural date. We chose a movie at Northlake Mall called "Sleepers" and had a very good time.

We hit it off, and after the movie, she suggested we go downtown to one of her favorite spots, Café Intermezzo. Let me be perfectly honest with you all: I did not have a lot of money, and it was a stretch for me to afford the movie, let alone popcorn and drinks. After the first part of our scheduled date, I had about ten dollars left, period!

The night was going very well, and the conversation was exhilarating. She ordered a specialty drink while I had water with lemon. As the outing was coming to a close, the waiter brought the bill and sat it by me as sweat beads started forming on my temples. I was praying she would grab it, and I would put up very little resistance. I also contemplated going to the restroom and bailing, but the latter was not an option when I realized I did not have my vehicle; we had driven her convertible, and my vehicle was at the apartment.

With extreme nervousness, I looked at the bill, and it was right under ten dollars. I exhaled. Then, I drove us back to my apartment and told her we would have to get together again soon. She agreed and said goodbye. As I stepped inside, my roommate's cousin was still up, and he asked me how everything went. I looked at him and said, "I am going to marry that girl one day."

Granddaddy's Farm

Financial difficulties during my childhood often pushed us to explore unconventional solutions. One memorable instance is connected to Grandaddy's farm. On the farm, we harvested sweet potatoes and collard greens, aiming to sell them in Lithonia, Georgia for extra income. Despite our optimism, challenges soon emerged. One day, the weight of the potatoes proved too much for the rented trailer, causing its axle to break on a Sunday. After that mishap our hopes for selling the harvested produce dwindled further upon our return. Despite our efforts to spread the word about our discounted offerings, the response was muted—the crickets seemed to be the only ones interested.

Undeterred, we approached a local grocery store, hoping to strike a deal. Unfortunately, our attempts were fruitless although they did allow us to sell the produce in the parking lot. Setting up shop at the back of my truck, we tried to make the extra money we desperately needed to survive. While I wish I could say we sold out and had a successful trip, it was not to be. Instead, we found ourselves with a surplus of potatoes and greens leading to inventive culinary creations for quite some time thereafter.

Growing up with very little instilled in me a deep appreciation for the small things in life, a value that has remained with me as I've grown older. Our upbringing taught us the importance of respect and carrying ourselves with dignity.

Back then, you never heard about Rosie Pearl's children getting into any trouble. Our country cousins would jokingly refer to us as "prisoners" because we could not go outside whenever we wanted as they could. We often found ourselves peering through the bed sheets that covered the windows of our single-wide trailer, yearning to be outside. Our mother kept a tight rein on us, perhaps to limit our exposure to negativity and preserve our innocence. Instead, she encouraged us to read books. There was a running joke that if Rosie Pearl's children were missing in a store, you could find them in the nearest book section. My affinity for books continues to this day, and they have been a constant source of joy and learning for me.

Fast Forward: Growing Pains

Through contacts my business partner RD knew, we met an older gentleman who was getting out of the lawn care business. He made a deal with us to take over many of his accounts. The additional accounts allowed us to have a dedicated day for the Campbellton Road Area in Southwest Atlanta. I thoroughly enjoyed interacting with the homeowners there. It was evident that they were very accomplished with generational wealth rather than just new money. They were not super rich, but well-off enough to have multiple generations of college graduates and social standing. One day marked a turning point in my thinking about the viability of our landscaping business. It shifted my paradigm, leading me to believe that the landscaping industry was not just a temporary pit stop until something better came along, but rather a promising career choice if approached properly.

That same day, a client approached me with an unexpected question: "Steve, can I have a word with you?" She then asked me what I wanted out of life and where I saw myself in the business. I stumbled around my answers, and she interjected, "Do you know you can make a million dollars cutting grass?" My response was reminiscent of Arnold from the 80's sitcom Different Strokes: "What you talkin' bout, Willis?!"

At that moment, a bright light went off in my head, and my direction forever changed.

The conversation with that customer elevated my thinking to a new level. I could not shake the realization of what I might be missing out on if I didn't give the business my all. RD and I decided to invest in a new trailer and upgrade our equipment, which I financed. In addition, we continued to refine our skills and expand our client base. With our growth, we were able to hire a couple of part-time employees. Things seemed to be progressing smoothly. During this time, my Christian faith deepened, fueling my determination to establish myself as a successful business owner.

One day, I received an unexpected call from the new deacon overseeing the facilities at our church. He delivered the news that the church was moving in a new direction and our services were no longer required. I was devastated on multiple levels. This contract was our main source of income and how we were paying the mortgage. I was furious beyond words!

I was overwhelmed with mixed emotions at the time, and RD was equally displeased. Despite this, we mustered the strength to head to the beach in search of some hopeful fun and relaxation. Even with a momentary break, my mind remained clouded throughout the weekend. Upon our return, there was a palpable void. My father, always the encourager, sent me a book titled *Who Moved My Cheese*. Little did I know, this book would reinvigorate my entrepreneurial spirit and propel me forward.

Shortly after receiving the phone call canceling our service with the church, I noticed that my partner and I no longer seemed to be on the same page. While I would arrive at jobs early and leave late, he would come late and leave early. It later became evident that he was laying the groundwork for continuing his schooling and eventually re-entering the military, which was understandable. The loss of the church contract was devastating for both of us. I scheduled a meeting with him one evening and expressed my belief that it was time for us to separate the business. His response was, "So you mean we should run two units so we can get more done?" I clarified, "No, I mean we dissolve Double "L" and run our businesses separately." We never had any arguments, and this was no different. Instead, he asked me about next steps. At that moment, I had not thought it through, but I said, "You can have everything except my truck, and I will start all over." This included the equipment that was financed in my name as he agreed to make the payments. When he asked how we would split the current customers, I replied, "You can have them all except my Pops and two other customers." As I said, I had not thought it through but had this overwhelming feeling that I would persevere and would not miss a beat.

Grass Clips

When you are determined and willing to do whatever is necessary to meet the challenges of life, you become stronger.

I was willing to do whatever it took to make the business work. After considering several options, I settled on a new business name: Bromell Manicured Lawns Inc. or BML Inc. for short. I invested in a new trailer and a mid-sized mower, taking my strong work ethic on the road to start rebuilding the business. By this time, I had developed the skills to attract customers through word of mouth. The business started to grow steadily. Additionally, I enlisted the help of a few friends who made calls and assisted me in generating more leads.

The business alone could not support all my financial obligations, so I took on a part-time job with a friend I met at church. Together, we began cleaning office buildings and retail spaces. We arrived at each location between two and three in the morning, completing our work by 6 a.m. to ensure the morning work shift was ready for the day ahead.

My tasks included cleaning some of the filthiest toilets imaginable and waxing and buffing floors that seemed to stretch endlessly. Despite feeling like I was taking a step back; this experience fueled my determination even more. I stuck to this routine for several months until I could afford to focus solely on the lawn business and support myself and my son. I was fueled by the words from the southwest Atlanta customer that kept ringing in my head "Steve, you can make a million dollars cutting grass. I know a guy who has done it."

A New Partnership

As I made my daily visits to the new storage unit, I noticed the steady stream of lawn contractors coming and going. My keen eye observed every detail: the trucks they drove, the trailers hitched behind them, and even their attire. Among them, a few individuals stood out. One was an older gentleman who exuded a sense of calm and efficiency. Despite the hustle and bustle around him, he appeared unfazed, and I found myself drawn to his demeanor. One day, I decided to strike up a conversation, and it led to an unexpected connection.

Grass Clips

Encounters with people in life can leave
unexpected impressions and lasting impacts.
It is crucial to approach each interaction with
patience and intuition, understanding the
potential significance it may hold.

We developed a strong friendship and a quasi-business mentorship, and through him, I learned the importance of strategic customer selection. He often emphasized his approach with the phrase, "I smack 'em," indicating his strategy for maximizing profit. Rather than pursuing numerous customers, he focused on a select few who valued integrity, character, and consistency. They were also willing to pay above market value. Eventually, he would introduce me to a pivotal figure in my early business journey—his son, later known as "Rich Man."

At that time, I'd roam around town, searching for guys mowing lawns. I'd discreetly park nearby, observing their techniques to glean tips and insights into their craft. I also picked up valuable advice on how to be more efficient and professional. Additionally, I noticed my newer competitors. Throughout DeKalb County, it seemed as if every telephone pole sported a sign for a company offering a full lawn service for $39.99 along with a phone number. It seemed like he must have had at least twenty pairs of stilts as the signs strategically were placed high up on the poles, requiring a tall ladder to remove them. They were scattered all over the place. Nonetheless, during this time, I was hitting a good stride in business and had recovered from the loss of the church account and the dissolution of the business partnership with Room Dog.

Chapter Three

MARRIAGE NETWORK

Wedding Bells

*W*ith a few thousand dollars saved, I felt it was time to take on more responsibility and commit to marriage. This decision was not taken lightly. Having grown up without a father figure for most of my life I understood the importance of making this decision thoughtfully and responsibly. Choosing a life partner was one of the most significant decisions as man I would make in my life.

I used my savings to visit a former customer, who owned the Diamond Warehouse, seeking assistance in creating a custom ring. With the help of brochures, I crafted a design that I knew Shawn would adore. I confided in a few close people about my plan, and on a Friday evening, I gathered my mother, brother, and little sisters to share the news: I was going to propose to Shawn A. Hightower. As the only unmarried child of my mother, the time was right. That evening at Cagney's, a restaurant I always admired but considered out of reach growing up, and by the piano bar, I popped the question—to which she joyfully with tears said, "yes."

At the time, I hadn't discussed much business or my aspirations for the future with Shawn. I recall a moment when she asked about my intentions for the future, and I downplayed what was truly in my heart, stating that I only wanted to do enough to take care of myself and my son, Michael Jr. Even when we got engaged, we didn't delve into the topic much further. I felt Shawn had a promising career as a news anchor in Charlotte, North Carolina and I assumed I would just uproot and move there. I believed I had what it took to start a new business and thrive, whether it was there or anywhere else.

Upon returning to work the following Monday after the proposal, I was filled with excitement and operating at a higher level of productivity. As I went about my tasks, I envisioned myself as a married man. With this newfound motivation, I began making plans to leave Atlanta. I arranged to inform my former customers, transport my equipment to Charlotte, and secure my first customer in the new area. The prospect of starting over was exhilarating, but I also recognized the importance of thorough planning given my existing experience.

I went through the process of identifying another business owner and transferring all my clients to him for a small monthly fee. Everything was going smoothly until Shawn dropped a bombshell: she no longer wanted to stay in Charlotte. Instead, she expressed a desire to return home to Atlanta. I was completely taken aback by this news, but I quickly adjusted my plans to accommodate her wishes.

Several months later, one evening my phone rang. It was my mother. Our conversation began with our usual pleasantries—her asking if I had been praying and taking care of myself. I assured her that I always prayed and was diligently working to ensure that I could take care of her one day. One of my dreams was to buy my mother a home and ensure that she never had to worry about anything financially again. I held onto the belief that the time would come for me to fulfill this dream one day.

Grass Clips

To all those reading or listening to this,
if it is within your power, I urge you not to delay doing
what you know needs to be done because you
never know what the future holds.

For years, I had been saving money, and during Christmas, I would give it to my mother. Throughout the year, I would help her here and there, but it was nowhere near what I wanted to do for her, especially with a small child to support myself.

She continued the conversation by revealing that her cancer had returned. The doctors had given a bleak prognosis. This news hit me hard considering her past battles with cancer and a stroke she had overcome. I remember feeling overwhelmed and helpless, grappling with the limited time we had left together. Ordinarily, I'd hold onto hope and remain optimistic, but something about her tone made me fear the worst. Without hesitation, I made plans to be by her side until she either recovered or reached the end of her life. I had a friend to call all my customers and tell them I had a family emergency and was not sure when I would return. Packing my bags, I embarked on the journey to South Carolina, sobbing and praying the entire way while seeking solace in inspirational music and sermons. Upon arriving home, in the middle of the night, my mother and I embraced tightly, cherishing every moment together.

On June 16, 2001, I married the stunning young lady whose car I parked nearly four years earlier; the one who had captured my attention with just one look. As I scanned the church, seeing my family and friends in the front row, I noticed three empty chairs deliberately left vacant. Exactly two months prior, my mother succumbed to lung cancer that had spread to her brain leaving an overwhelming void in my heart. The other two chairs were reserved in honor of my beloved grandmother with whom I had lived with for several years, and Willie Earl Bromell, my father.

Before my mother's passing, Shawn and I had purchased a new home in Lithonia, Georgia, but we made an agreement to only move in once we were married. All our belongings had been relocated before the wedding, so upon our return, we settled in immediately. We didn't plan a honeymoon because I knew I needed to get back to work to generate income. We went straight into growth mode focusing on how to support our new household and my son. The next few years were tough with me working tirelessly during the spring, summer, and part of the fall. During slower times when customers cut back on services, I would return to South Carolina to work with my best friend laying tile to cover our expenses.

The Network

As time passed, I couldn't help but notice the prevalence of the $39.99 Lawn Care signs everywhere. I found myself pondering who this person was and why he didn't just round up the price to forty dollars per service! One day, while performing maintenance on my equipment at my assigned storage unit, a gentleman pulled up and struck up a conversation. He asked how I was doing. I replied positively, asking about him in return. After introducing ourselves, he mentioned he was working on a significant opportunity and asked if I would be interested in joining. Intrigued by the prospect of a large opportunity, I eagerly expressed my interest in hearing more.

As the pieces of the puzzle fell into place, I realized that he was the mastermind behind the $39.99 Lawn Care operation! He explained that while the new deal he was working on was not finalized yet, he was preparing for it as if it were. He outlined his strategy and how I could be involved. Despite my initial excitement, I had to decline his offer, but asked him to keep me in mind for future opportunities. A few weeks later, I watched in awe as he secured a million-dollar contract. Up until that point, I had not known anyone in the lawn care industry with more than two trucks and a handful of employees. His success set a new benchmark for my aspirations, and he quickly became the standard by which I measured my goals.

I declined his offer because I did not feel ready to partner on a project of that scale at the time. Even though I declined, the opportunity sparked a hunger for success within me and provided me with a role model. A few weeks later, while at the storage unit, another gentleman approached me who would become invaluable to me for many years to come. He was starting a group called The Lawn Management Network, also known as The Network. This collective of lawn care business owners met monthly to share ideas, resources, opportunities, and business lessons. Reflecting on my journey in this industry, I can identify three pivotal events. The first was marrying Shawn, the second was the southwest Atlanta customer challenging me to pursue success in lawn care, and the third was joining The Network.

The Network was founded and supported directly by what I would later refer to as the godfathers and one godmother of the lawn care industry—some of the top owners within The Network. They possessed the finest equipment, trucks, and the most employees. As well as what appeared to be exceptional business acumen. I meticulously observed their every move, learning valuable lessons along the way. The Network exposed me to more than one hundred companies at its peak, enabling me to learn from them and forge lasting relationships.

Embarking on a journey in the business world often begins with a dream and a burning desire. Without proper planning, many dive in hastily, leading to years of turmoil and costly mistakes.

Let me be clear: I'm not denigrating this approach—it's one I've taken myself. It's been a source of growth, offering me a roadmap of what not to do. Obtaining guidance from the outset is unquestionably a better choice.

My first meeting with The Network was a transformative experience igniting growth in my mind and spirit. We convened at a Shoney's on Wesley Chapel Road in Decatur, Georgia. To my surprise, each meeting commenced with prayer. As I sat in the back, I marveled at how these businessmen and women, who owned various lawn care and non-lawn care businesses *(including a tree service)* openly acknowledged their commitment to serving God first. The agenda was rich with informative discussions on a variety of business topics, but the highlight was undoubtedly the networking and relationship-building opportunities. Though I remained silent during the first meeting, at the second one, they sought my input on my business activities.

At that time, my wife and I were about six months pregnant with our first child. We had no insurance and no significant income. Shawn had not worked outside of our lawn care business since leaving Charlotte. With a little one on the way, it seemed like additional employment for her would not be an option for a while. Little did I know at the time, she would never work outside of what we would build together!

During my upbringing, we constantly found ourselves borrowing and essentially resorting to what felt like begging from others. Whether it was asking for food, used clothes, rides to and from places, or a place to live, it seemed there was no end to it. I made a vow never to have to ask people for things or rely on the government to survive. I decided that if I had breath in my body and was physically capable, I would work my fingers to the bone to support myself and my family.

At the end of my second meeting at The Network, I was asked to share what I was doing and where I was headed in business. Like most people, I gave a surface response saying everything was good. But then I decided to get real. I asked everyone to pray for me because my wife was pregnant; we had no health insurance, and quite frankly, I didn't know how we would make it.

Grass Clips

If you are not bold enough to knock on the door, people will not know you want to be let in.

What followed was significant. The men and women all rose from their seats, extending their hands toward me in prayer. After exchanging handshakes and words of encouragement, I left. While driving back to our storage unit, I received a phone call instructing me to go to the Bank of America on Wesley Chapel Road and ask for a specific lady as she had something for me. Though hesitant, I obeyed. To my surprise, there was a check waiting for me in the amount of $1,000. This unexpected act of kindness came from none other than the $39.99 Lawn Care Guy. His generosity strengthened my faith, and resilience, and ultimately sharpened my determination.

Grass Clips

A single act of kindness has the
potential to yield a lifetime of blessings,
not only for yourself, but for others as well!

Seeds planted in fertile soil can yield an endless harvest especially when nurtured with kindness. That single act filled gaps in our lives at the time and inspired me to pay it forward to countless others in the years that followed. In The Network, everyone shared a common desire for growth and success. The environment was infused with a genuine faith-driven ethos that facilitated the exploration of one's purpose in Christ. Observing my peers in the same industry, I noticed a myriad of qualities that contributed to their success: their communication style, character, willingness to help others, attire, and openness in sharing business insights. Additionally, I found it fascinating to observe the diverse array of vehicles employed for their businesses.

At that time, most individuals had what we commonly referred to as the "truck and trailer" setup. One day, a fellow member of The Network arrived with an exceptionally clean Dodge. It was a white dually truck with an enclosed trailer adorned with a striking name on its sides. Instantly, I felt the need to elevate my vehicle's professional appearance as well. Instead of emulating this individual's setup "To a T," I opted for a slightly different approach. He would later become a close friend.

I discussed this with my business partner and wife, Shawn, and we decided to search for a new vehicle. Eventually, we settled on a Black Dodge Ram 1500 and acquired a black enclosed trailer. Remarkably, all of this happened within a year of receiving that initial seed money from the $39.99 Lawn Care Guy.

As a newly married man grappling with the responsibilities of running a household and still grieving the loss of my mother, I found myself cutting grass and shedding tears simultaneously on many days. When my mother initially called me to tell me she was sick I ended up staying in South Carolina for a couple of months. Only one client decided to go elsewhere for services! Those tears served as a catalyst, urging me to tap into my inner strength and recognize that I was not meant to merely exist in this world but to strive for excellence in everything I did. On one occasion, while mowing a client's lawn, the sadness over my mother's passing weighed heavily on me. I could not shake the regret of not expressing my feelings or asking the questions I had while she was still alive.

Grass Clips

Do not squander your time in pursuit of things,
only to neglect the people for whom
you are seeking them.

I was so engrossed in chasing my dreams that I overlooked something we all tend to take for granted: time. None of us knows when our time will run out, but we do know it's finite.

It is crucial to seize every opportunity to express love to those close to you. My client encouraged me to honor my mother's memory by helping others and achieving my goals. He also gifted me a book that had brought him solace when his mother had passed away. That book became a source of reconciliation and healing for me as well. During our conversations, he shared his dreams and aspirations. Years later, I was blessed to see a billboard advertising the business he once dreamt of starting, his dream had become a reality.

A Taste of Commercial Contracts

The first person I connected with in the storage area had a son who also owned a landscaping company. He possessed a remarkable talent for sales and securing business opportunities, particularly in government contracting, much like the $39.99 Lawn Care Guy. Through our interactions at networking events and conversations at the storage facility, we developed a friend-ship. Most of the individuals I knew in the industry primarily focused on residential maintenance tasks like cutting grass, edging, trimming, hedge trimming, and property cleanup. On the other hand, my friend ventured into commercial contracts, securing projects such as servicing a college campus.

I joined him once a week for a few hours, bringing along my mower to ensure we had enough equipment for the job. Together, we worked tirelessly, rotating on short breaks to keep the mowers running continuously. Despite the challenging workload, those were exhilarating times fueled by our youth and determination. Looking back, I'm still amazed that we managed to complete the entire college campus maintenance with just three people in eight hours. It was a testament to our dedication and teamwork.

The meetings at Shoney's continued, and The Network expanded, providing me with invaluable education. As a sign of progress, the meetings transitioned to evenings and diversified in terms of venues, ranging from schools to office buildings. Each gathering became an anticipated event for me, particularly when we began inviting guest speakers to address the members.

We were fortunate to host professionals from various fields including accountants, bankers, financial services experts, insurance agents, and equipment dealers. Their presentations enlightened us on a range of topics, from the importance of proper insurance coverage to strategic financial leveraging for business growth. I diligently took notes and absorbed every detail, recognizing the potential for our businesses to flourish through informed decision-making and strategic partnerships.

Most individuals entering the industry aimed to support themselves or supplement their family income rather than viewing it as a long-term career. For me, the statement from our southwest Atlanta client resonated in my mind. "Steve, do you know you can make a million dollars cutting grass?" I replied, "No ma'am, I never thought about it like that." Yet, over time, I began to believe that such success was possible, even if I was not earning over $40k a year at the time.

During one of our meetings, it was announced that The Network would be relocating to its first building in Decatur, Georgia. The building, a two-story structure, was nestled on a private road, keeping it secluded from the main road and passing traffic. This aspect was advantageous as it provided ample space for various businesses and their equipment. With several conference rooms, multiple offices, warehouse space, and a few acres of parking areas, the property offered extensive amenities. Upstairs, our business and prayer meetings would take place, and we even conducted interviews with potential employees in the conference rooms. One of the most memorable experiences was our joint interview sessions. Through our network and collaborative efforts, The Network was approached by The Southeastern Flower Show to participate in an exhibit for the annual Flower Show held at the Georgia World Congress Center in Downtown Atlanta.

BML Inc. was chosen to be part of the five-member team representing The Network. As we began planning and discussing concepts and designs, I realized that I was more of a lawn maintenance provider than a landscaper, so many of their ideas went over my head. They talked about force blooming, eco-friendly ponds, textured plantings, hardscapes, and more. When they mentioned hardscapes and the need for outdoor tiling, I realized that I could be helpful in that area due to my experience laying tile with my best friend in South Carolina. The next challenge was determining our theme.

As I contemplated the dilemma, I couldn't shake the significance of being asked to participate in this Flower Show. Then, like a sudden rainbow across the sky after a storm, the idea struck me instantaneously. Let's present something that acknowledges our past while announcing our presence! And so, I proposed the title: "In the Back of the Shack." The entrance would resemble a typical slave quarter, but as you entered through the back door, you would be greeted with stunning modern landscape designs. It was a stroke of brilliance and earned us several awards, opening doors to greater opportunities for advertising and marketing.

"Who wouldn't want to hire an award-winning company?" I thought to myself. Landing in a few magazines and newspapers due to our project gave the Lawn Management Network even more exposure. The team represented very well, along with our wives, during the unveiling of "In the Back of The Shack." Unfortunately, as much as I had hoped and believed, the Network did not stand the test of time. After several years, it seemingly imploded. I often wonder just what we would have accomplished had we kept it together and not allowed the infighting, jealousy, and lack of focus to overtake it. Despite it all, I gained lifelong relationships.

The Aftermath

One day, we received a call to bid on a new landscape project at a local church. Fueled by our recent awards and the belief that we could accomplish anything, we eagerly agreed to provide a quote. Upon receiving the scope of work, I had the bright idea to present a design with before and after pictures. Despite lacking professional training in design, I was confident that I could do it, so I purchased a design CD-ROM. But I didn't stop there. I decided to involve Shawn, my wife, in presenting the plan. Using the CD-ROM, I crafted a new landscape plan for the potential client, complete with all the necessary elements like new grass, shrubs, trees, mulch, and flowers, along with cars in the parking lot, and people going inside the church to make it look realistic. I thoroughly briefed Shawn on potential questions and appropriate answers, as well as different landscape terms to use that would be practical and easily understood.

On the day of the meeting, I was nervous about sending her in alone, but I was also confident in her ability to handle herself. Despite my apprehension, she delivered a fantastic presentation; however, the church ultimately chose to go with another company. Even though we did not win the bid, I remained grateful for the opportunity. I believed that any exposure and opportunity would be beneficial for our brand.

Grass Clips

Every setback carries growth potential
if you glean lessons from it.

Through that experience, we gained valuable insights. We committed to building our brand steadily, prioritizing each client for long-term growth. Strategy meetings became regular occurrences. We meticulously outlined not just our current business status, but also our precise goals for the future.

In the pursuit of rapid business growth,
it's easy to become unfocused and remain in a
state of mediocrity longer than needed.
Business owners must cultivate clarity and maintain
a clear focus to reach their desired goals.
Preparation becomes their springboard to success,
enabling them to navigate challenges effectively
and seize opportunities with confidence.

The Power of a Helping Hand

One day, while driving between clients, I received a call from the church to whom we had presented our landscaping services months prior. The client expressed discontent with the service provided by the company they chose and sought our expertise to improve it. After discussing options, we agreed on immediate steps such as a thorough clean-up and adding flowers and mulch. I then reached out to the $39.99 Lawn Care Guy, now known to me as Eagle, for advice. His response was swift: "Steve, change into your manager khakis and polo, and meet us at the church." What followed was nothing short of remarkable. Within hours, five or more landscaping companies converged at the site, armed with bobcats, dump trucks, pine straw, mulch, flowers, mowers, edgers, trimmers, blowers, and ample manpower to swiftly transform the property in quick order.

The impact of our collective effort on that property left the management speechless. Much of what we accomplished that day was made possible by the relationships and seeds of goodwill developed through former members of The Network. Not only did we secure the contract on the spot, but we also maintained a fruitful partnership with the client for more than fifteen years. An amusing anecdote from the experience was our unexpected task of removing over 200 bales of straw. It was not desired by the client, as he had an aversion to pine straw. Undeterred, we approached the task with enthusiasm and replaced it with red mulch, which received the owner's approval! This experience taught us a valuable lesson: even when offering something for free, it is crucial to research and ensure your actions align with the recipient's preferences. The only exception to this rule is money as it grants people the freedom to acquire what they desire.

As mentioned earlier, when The Network disbanded, many businesses went their separate ways, and there was little contact afterward. Before its dissolution, the $39.99 Lawn Care Guy had assembled a group known as The Eagles. The group's purpose was to foster deeper relationships with God and to provide mutual encouragement in business endeavors. He acknowledged at the outset that he wasn't sure of all that God wanted from them, but they approached it with optimism and high expectations. We would gather for fellowship and prayer and to share dreams and ideas about their futures.

My spiritual journey began to take precedence over my business aspirations. Initially, I struggled to keep the two separate, but eventually, I realized they were intertwined. Through consistent engagement with Bible study, motivational literature, recordings, conferences, and sermons, I felt a deepening connection with God and a growing sense of future success. The Eagles met for weekly Bible study sessions at a local church followed by enriching lunch discussions. These gatherings fueled my hunger for spiritual growth and readiness to follow wherever God led me. It's no coincidence that my business expertise flourished during this period, especially with the introduction to government contracting by Rich Man. This opened new opportunities for us.

Chapter Four

WEIGHTY THEFT

An Unexpected Gift

One day, I had a revelation: wanting success wasn't enough; I needed a solid plan to achieve what I believed was meant for me. So, I started writing out my plan as a prayer. Every day, I would sit in my truck, reading it, meditating on it, and speaking it aloud. Slowly but surely, I began to believe in it wholeheartedly! I was fueled by a passion for my dream. The only caveat? I had no earthly idea how long it would take to reach what I envisioned as success.

With my dreams soaring high, another bright idea struck me. I persuaded my wife, also my business partner, that it was time for us to elevate our game and invest in a commercial truck. Up until then, most people in the business relied on the traditional pick-up truck and trailer setup. I, on the other hand, believed we could minimize liability and simplify operations by opting for a commercial truck. As part of my spiritual growth, I began honing my envisioning skills. I not only thought about what I wanted, but also visualized it through pictures. I stumbled upon the perfect vehicle that matched my vision: an Isuzu NPR 14' Box Truck.

I recalled meeting a graphic designer at one of our networking meetings, so I reached out to him and asked if he could take a picture of the truck and incorporate our logo onto it. This would be a significant upgrade for our business. The image of the truck with the logo began to materialize into reality. Shortly after, my Pops sold his house in Southwest Atlanta and expressed his desire to invest in our business. His unwavering belief in me further bolstered my confidence.

We made a strategic decision to invest in the future of our commercial lawn maintenance business, recognizing that growth would require various resources including cash flow, investable funds, insurance, sweat equity, and manpower. With the generous seed money from my father, we allocated our financial resources toward obtaining the necessary insurance for government contracting, hiring an accountant, and investing the remainder in upgrading our equipment. Although I was eager to acquire the box truck, I had a gut feeling that waiting for the right timing would yield a better return in the long term, especially considering our limited initial investment capital of about $5,000.

Indeed, business is not about short-term rewards but long-term success. Many entrepreneurs fall into the trap of the "I deserve" or "I can't wait syndrome," which can lead to a losing strategy. By embracing delayed gratification and adopting a mindset focused on measured growth, success becomes inevitable. We made the conscious decision to hunker down and focus on becoming more efficient with what we had. I recognized that lawn maintenance often had a negative perception and was seen as an unattractive occupation. Despite this, in my vision, I aimed to run our business like any successful corporation, with a strong emphasis on professionalism and excellence.

Implementing the *Monthly Manicure Newsletter* was one of the strategies we adopted to enhance our customer engagement. This newsletter provided valuable tips and insights for our customers, including my favorite segment, *Steve's Manicured Moment*, which served as an inspiration column. During estimates, I made it a point to present myself professionally, dressed in khakis and a nice polo, and equipped with a comprehensive book showcasing our portfolio of work. Additionally, I ensured all necessary insurance policies, including general liability, auto insurance, and workers comp, were readily available. I believed that demonstrating our legitimacy in this manner would convey our professionalism and the quality of service our potential clients could expect. With these efforts, BML Inc. was gaining momentum and experiencing growth.

Running a business is akin to raising children; you cradle them in your hands at birth, and then the journey of struggles and joys unfolds over time. Before you know it, they're walking, talking, and asking for the car keys. Similarly, a business grows and evolves, and one day you find yourself looking back, wondering where all the time went. In just five years of marriage, we had progressed from a Ford Ranger with an open trailer to a sleek black F-350 dually accompanied by an enclosed black trailer adorned with eye-catching yellow and green graphics.

The Box Truck

Later, we finally acquired the longed-for box truck. After finding the perfect one, we went to the dealership to seal the deal. Surprisingly, the transaction went smoothly, one of the smoothest I had ever experienced when it came to financing a purchase. With the down payment made, I proudly drove our first commercial vehicle back to our storage area. Most box trucks at the time came equipped with lift gates, which typically cost an additional $600 or more to remove and dispose of.

I decided to keep it on the truck for the time being until we could have it removed and replaced with what is known as a dovetail, which would allow us to safely transport lawn equipment on the back of the truck.

Nonetheless, we acquired the box truck that matched our enclosed trailer, solidifying our identity as a boutique, high-end lawn care provider. Our slogan, "We Manicure Lawns," became a staple banner on all our advertisements, further establishing our brand identity.

Without a moment's doubt, I can unequivocally say that every good thing in my life is solely attributed to my faith in God. Through every trial, every challenge of growth, every rejection, every moment of lacking, every sleepless night, every tear shed while cutting grass, every doubt about my decisions, and every instance when it felt like the world was against me, my faith has been my unwavering anchor.

Let me paint a vivid picture for you: Picture this—you've just purchased this vehicle, right? But here's the kicker: there's no solid business rationale to justify such a splurge on a truck.

Sounds crazy, huh? Yet, deep down, I sensed something profound—a divine whisper nudging me forward. It was as if God Himself was saying, "Now's the time." And let me tell you, I was determined to heed His call. Now, you'd think that after a few months of no extra work rolling in, my faith would waver, right? But not a chance. I remained resolute, steadfast in my belief that blessings await those who have faith—faith that moves mountains, faith that acts.

So, guess what I did? I acted. I realized that to move forward, I needed to make some changes. And wouldn't you know it, fate intervened. My neighbor, a fellow entrepreneur and newfound friend, happened to be in the graphics business. Serendipitous, right? One day, as he was gearing up to tackle some lawns, I caught him for a quick chat.

"Hey, mind sparing a few minutes?" I asked eagerly. He obliged, and I seized the opportunity to share my vision for the business with him. I described the kind of logos I envisioned, one that exuded elegance and visual appeal. I tossed around a couple of ideas, suggesting one incorporating a golf course hole-in-one to symbolize pristine putting green lawns, and another that was so brilliantly simple it would leave you in awe. After a few days, he presented me with two designs and I was amazed—I never knew I had access to such talent.

Thanks to my Pops who knew a diverse group of people in varying industries, we put the designs to the test, sending them out to the focus group for votes. The outcome? We settled on a logo that epitomized simplicity. And with that decision made, we embarked on the journey of refining our company brand's image. I was particularly fond of our base colors: sleek black vehicles adorned with vibrant yellow and green lettering. The BML logo took center stage, featuring bold letters with a striking 3D effect, surrounded by delicate cat tails.

We decided to go all out with our branding, opting for hats emblazoned solely with the BML lettering, reminiscent of the iconic FBI hats. I believed that projecting a polished image would open doors to greater opportunities and expansion for our business. Soon enough, our branding extended beyond hats to include t-shirts, sweatshirts, and even turning our vehicles into rolling billboards. And you know what? It paid off!

With our professional appearance in place, the only missing piece of the puzzle was securing the business to match. I've always been a dreamer, someone unafraid to push the boundaries of convention. So, when I heard about the annual trade show for lawn equipment dealers, hosted by none other than Howard Brothers—the biggest event of its kind in metro Atlanta—I knew it was time to make my mark. I'd never attended such a show before, but I sensed that this year was different; this year, I needed to make a grand entrance.

Not an assertion of superiority, but rather a stirring indication that we were on the right track, I decided to take a bold step. I enlisted the help of a few individuals, offering them lunch in exchange for simply attending the event wearing our branded sweatshirts. My rationale was simple: the more people who spotted our logo, the more it would signal professionalism and credibility. And you know what? It didn't take long for curiosity to stir as attendees began inquiring about our identity.

Reflecting on it now, I find it amusing—I've always preferred operating behind the scenes, letting the name speak louder than any personal recognition. Shortly after the trade show, we inked a contract that not only filled our truck to capacity but also generated overflow work that had to be outsourced to one of our partners. It felt like we were hitting our stride, but little did I know, there was a storm brewing on the horizon, one I hadn't anticipated.

Feeling the need to stay ahead of the game, I made sure to print out the daily schedules for the truck and headed to the storage unit early one morning. I planned to leave the schedules inside for our crew leader since I wouldn't be there in person to greet him as usual.

As I reached the storage unit and made my way to the back of the parking lot where we kept the box truck and trailer, I was met with a shocking sight—the truck was gone. It was as if a sinking feeling had settled in my gut as I surveyed the scene, noticing the gate had been cut wide open.

The others arrived shortly thereafter, and instead of giving in to frustration or anger, we took a different approach. After calling 911, we didn't engage in complaints, screams, curses, or finger-pointing. Instead, we became authoritative prayer warriors, rallying together for one of the most powerful prayer sessions I've ever experienced. There we stood, in that parking lot, missing tens of thousands of dollars' worth of stolen equipment, but united in faith and determination.

As the police arrived, their bafflement was palpable. How could we, a group of individuals who had just suffered a significant theft, be in such high spirits? Little did they know our faith had been bolstered to even greater heights by the events of that day. And what unfolded next only served to reinforce it. After gathering ourselves, we decided to head out for breakfast to regroup and contemplate our next steps. Over breakfast, I found myself pondering our predicament. While it was reassuring to know that we had insurance coverage for everything that was stolen, the harsh reality was that insurance companies do not exactly operate at lightning speed. We were facing a pressing need for our equipment and truck to fulfill our contractual obligations and keep our business moving forward.

There was a trusted equipment dealer in our area that many in the industry relied on: Cowan Ace Hardware. Uncertain of what to expect, I reached out and spoke to their main salesman. As soon as I mentioned my name, he immediately recognized it and remarked on my good reputation.

With a heavy heart, I explained the situation, detailing the theft of our equipment. Without hesitation, he offered a solution: if we had a trailer, he would fill it with whatever equipment we needed. Concerned about the financial burden, I mentioned our lack of funds to make such a purchase. His response was reassuring—he told me not to worry. Once the insurance company compensated us, we could settle the bill.

Several months later, to our astonishment, our stolen truck was recovered—miraculously pristine, with nothing but a thin layer of dust in the back. Unfortunately, our equipment remained elusive, nowhere to be found despite our hopes. Yet, amidst this disappointment, a silver lining emerged. The insurance company finally came through, sending us a check to compensate for the stolen equipment. With this financial relief, we were able to fulfill our promise to Cowan Ace Hardware, repaying them in full for their remarkable generosity and unwavering trust.

Grass Clips

Every move made toward your goals serves as
progress toward achieving your dreams!

At times in life, unforeseen events unfold, appearing inexplicable in the moment but later revealed as necessary setbacks propelling us forward. In response to the theft, I took precautions by ensuring all our equipment was stored at a facility overnight and never leaving the work truck at home. We diligently removed all mowers and power tools every evening, securely storing them in a locked unit until the next day. One evening, exhausted and running late, I made a rare exception. Instead of making the trek to the storage facility, I chose to keep the truck in the driveway for just one night. It was packed to the brim with equipment requiring me to rearrange items just to secure the door closed.

That decision turned out to be both a blessing and a curse. At the time, my wife had set up a makeshift office upstairs near our bedroom, where she often worked late into the night while our baby boy slept soundly. Our loyal companion, Dallas Cowboy, a big Golden Retriever with a formidable bark, always kept watch over her, following her wherever she went. Between 2 to 3 a.m., Dallas Cowboy's growls pierced the silence signaling something amiss. His warning preceded a persistent knocking sound, which initially felt like a fragment of a dream in my deep sleep until it jolted me awake alongside the echoing growls.

Peering out of the window, I noticed the door to our box truck slightly ajar—a sight that sent chills down my spine considering I had securely locked it when I parked. In a heartbeat, I grabbed my makeshift weapon and flung open the door, confronting the intruders with a stern warning: "If you want to live to see another day, I suggest you run."

The police were promptly summoned, but it seemed the would-be thieves heard our commotion and fled the scene, leaving behind our vehicle filled with the fruits of our labor and a busted ignition housing. It was a chilling reminder of the fragility of security and the value of vigilance.

After such a harrowing experience, sleep eluded me, and I stayed awake for the remainder of the night. Surprisingly, when I reached out to my neighbor down the street, he answered my call and promptly met me at my house—an act of kindness for which I was immensely grateful. Without any clear reason, we felt compelled that night to embark on a journey through town, searching for suitable office space.

I explained to him the urgent need for a secure location where we could not only park our truck but also have office facilities. We felt an eerie sense of being watched and trailed, intensifying our apprehension about potential thefts lurking in the shadows. As we navigated the streets that night, my neighbor introduced me to unfamiliar areas, which would later prove instrumental in our business endeavors. Strangely, what initially appeared as a setback sparked a newfound determination within us, driving us to take another bold step forward on our path to success.

We stumbled upon two potential locations that seemed

suitable for a stand-alone office with warehouse space. The first one I visited caught me off guard when the landlord mentioned we'd need to sign a triple net lease. Frankly, I had no clue what that entailed. Despite the prime location and apparent potential, further research revealed that such a lease would not be advantageous for us, so we decided to move on.

Less than a mile away, we discovered another property boasting two offices, a conference room, a spacious double foyer, and a warehouse complete with an industrial roll-up door. In an instant, it felt like we had stumbled upon the perfect spot! I wasted no time in reaching out to the landlord, arranging a walk-through, and skillfully negotiating the lease rates. The rest, as they say, is history.

Just before putting pen to paper, I requested another walk-through from the landlord, who graciously entrusted us with a key, allowing us unrestricted access to the vacant building. What followed next would leave an indelible mark on our journey in that space—we prayed. With heartfelt petitions, we sought not only our ability to meet our lease obligations faithfully and with integrity but also an abundance of growth, business expansion, and blessings upon the landlord and his family.

As we immersed ourselves in prayer, the landlord unexpectedly walked in, visibly taken aback by our presence.

Little did he know, this humble act of faith would set the tone for our tenure in that building. For nearly a decade, we remained steadfast tenants, never once faltering in our commitment to meet our lease payments promptly, regardless of the challenges we faced.

Grass Clips

In the unpredictable journey of business,
you will encounter numerous twists and turns,
highs, and lows. Yet, if you anchor yourself
with faith, it becomes a stabilizing force that
may pull you, but never uproot you
from your destined path.

From Residential to Commercial

From then until now, my anchor has remained steadfastly rooted in my faith and reliance on God. You might wonder what that truly means to me. To put it simply, it's about surrendering self-centered desires and embracing something greater—a creative force that orchestrates opportunities far more enduring and sustaining than what one could achieve alone.

While I was attending to one of our customers, a car abruptly halted in the middle of the road. The driver gestured for me to approach the driver's side window. "Excuse me, sir," she said, "When you're finished over there, could you come across the street to my house and look at my lawn?" I enthusiastically agreed, assuring her that I would be there as soon as I completed my current task. After wrapping up the property I was working on, I made my way to the woman's house and knocked on her door. She welcomed me warmly and expressed her admiration for the work I was doing for her neighbor across the street. Then, she explained, she needed a gardener, not just someone who cuts grass. Slightly perplexed, I asked her to clarify the specific services she required.

Her lawn didn't present the typical challenges I encountered with most initial services. When she asked if I had experience using a reel mower, I must admit, I was initially unfamiliar with the term. My lack of knowledge didn't last for long. Utilizing a reel mower allowed us to offer a specialized service that commanded a higher price, required meticulous attention to detail, and ultimately delivered an exceptional finish. It was a game-changer for us, opening doors to new opportunities and setting us up to having a niche in the lawn care industry.

Business became an extraordinary journey of continual learning and discovery; a journey characterized by pivots and self-reinvention. Following insightful discussions with Shawn, we confronted some tough realities. Despite years of operation, we found ourselves struggling, particularly during the winter months. Determined to turn the tide, we made bold decisions.

To begin, we resolved to exclusively take on weekly customers. Secondly, we implemented a policy requiring all customers to sign a yearly contract and make monthly payments in advance. We recognized the risks of these changes, yet we were confident in the quality of our work. We understood that while we might lose some customers, those departures would lead to gains ultimately. We focused on cultivating relationships with clients who valued our services and were committed for the long term.

As anticipated, while some customers chose to leave, the majority opted to stay, and we even began to attract new clients. Our strategy was simple: by operating in a more businesslike, even corporate manner, we aimed to appeal to clients who were similarly business-minded and wouldn't hesitate to adhere to our terms.

Moreover, our decision to relocate to a new central location paid off handsomely. It allowed us to market our services more effectively in the surrounding area. And the results? Well, they spoke for themselves—it worked!

Givers Are Winners

"Steve, call Boyd! Steve, call Boyd!" This urgent message was left on my answering service by one of our esteemed clients, his distinct island accent echoing in my mind. As I expanded our high-end residential business, my aim was always to give back to society. Yet, a challenge arose: our funds were limited. Nonetheless, I firmly believe that giving stems from the heart, and for those willing to sow, opportunities arise.

After placing flyers in a local publication, Boyd reached out to me, and during our conversation, I provided an estimate for our services. They were incredibly pleasant, and as I sat at their kitchen table, I felt confident in my presentation to them. As I bid them farewell, they expressed their intention to review everything and promised to call me later with their decision. A few days passed before they reached out, delivering the disappointing news that, despite their admiration for our presentation, they simply couldn't afford our services at the moment. Grateful for the opportunity, I thanked them and left the door open for future possibilities, urging them to reach out if their circumstances changed.

As I hung up the phone, memories of my grandmother flooded my mind, her nurturing love and selflessness echoing in my heart. Strikingly, the wife reminded me of my grandmother, evoking a deep sense of connection and compassion. The next time I found myself in their neighborhood, I pulled up to the curb by their home and made a spontaneous decision:

I would cut their grass for free. This simple act marked the beginning of a tradition for us—a commitment to provide a free service to a deserving client each year. For us, the absence of money would not be a barrier to giving back using our time and talents.

Each time I tended to their lawn, I approached it with the utmost care and diligence, treating it as if it belonged to the most esteemed and valued customer in the world. It was not just about cutting grass; it was about manicuring it to perfection, a labor of love that honored their kindness and reflected our deepest values. Initially, I'm certain they were startled by the sudden roar of the mower in their yard. They emerged from their door, always hand in hand, waving and calling out my name. Pausing my work, I approached them, and they inquired, "What are you doing?" With a smile, I replied, "Taking care of your lawn, and it's completely free!" Their reaction was one of surprise—not just at the immediate service but also at the commitment I made to provide it for the entire year without charge.

Grass Clips

As you navigate the journey towards success,
remember that significance often begins with simplicity.
One act of kindness, no matter how small,
holds immense power and impact.

The Pre-bid Meeting

With a blend of commercial and high-end residential clients, our business was beginning to take shape, in line with my vision. We had expanded to three box trucks, each operating at full capacity, yet I yearned for even greater growth. On a slow day before our move to a new office, I found myself cruising around town, admiring various landscapes and techniques. It was during this leisurely drive that my Nextel chirped to life— an associate inquiring about my whereabouts. I casually replied that I was just exploring different parts of town.

Curiously, my associate mentioned that he was planning to attend a mandatory pre-bid meeting and invited me to attend as well. Little did I know that this seemingly simple invitation would turn out to be one of the most significant moments in my entire journey as a business owner.

The pre-bid meeting was bustling with what seemed like a crowd of at least a hundred people hailing from various locations. While I had attended bid meetings in the past, none had quite the same scale of work as this one. The packet distributed was impressively thick, and the sign-in sheet stretched on endlessly. As I signed in under our company name, I could not help but steal glances at some of the other names on the list. To my surprise, there were only a handful that I recognized—most were unfamiliar to me.

The meeting kicked off with an introduction from the organizing entity, followed by a concise overview of the day's agenda. With the room packed to capacity, many attendees were left standing—a promising sign for securing responses, especially for a government contract.

Once the agenda was covered, participants were asked to introduce themselves, stating their names and company affiliations. It was an enlightening experience to listen to each company's introduction. Their descriptions were remarkably detailed, accompanied by visual aids showcasing their areas of expertise and, at times, highlighting their challenges with vivid imagery. What truly captivated me were the remarks and inquiries posed by what appeared to be the key players in the industry. Their insights and questions underscored the significance of this gathering and hinted at the competitive landscape awaiting those vying for the contract.

After the meeting adjourned, I made my way through the small gatherings outside, scanning the faces until I spotted one of the owners from The Show, along with a few other acquaintances from The Network. The Show always intrigued me—I marveled at their operations and often found myself inspired by their achievements, as they embodied the limitless potential of the industry.

As I later learned, their primary focus lay in highway work—an endeavor that demanded immense scale and expertise to navigate the challenges inherent in such projects. Yet, despite the complexities of their operations, they exuded a remarkable level of knowledge and business acumen, leaving me in awe of their capabilities—which is why I nicknamed them "The Show."

During a conversation at one of the trade shows, I sought guidance and insights from one of the owners, hoping to glean valuable knowledge from an industry leader. Nevertheless, as is common in business circles, many individuals maintain a guarded demeanor, often withholding information or being somewhat evasive when it comes to discussing their strategies. While there was nothing overtly negative about the interaction, I didn't quite feel the warmth and openness I had hoped for at the time. Yet, my journey would lead me to forge a relationship with another owner—one that would prove to be immensely beneficial in the years to come.

Moreover, as I stood outside the pre-bid location, a surge of determination coursed through me, prompting me to exclaim, "We can do this!" Ideas began to crystallize in my mind, and I realized that putting a plan into action would not take much time at all. Eager to gather more insights, I engaged in conversations, asking questions and making observations. I made sure to exchange contact information with everyone I spoke to. Before leaving, I expressed my confidence to those around me, affirming my belief that we could indeed tackle this challenge and succeed.

I proposed a meeting in the following days and gauged the interest of those I had connected with. Deep down, I believed that securing the involvement of an individual from "The Show," who possessed firsthand experience in the field, would greatly bolster our chances of success. Due to some internal business issues, they were no longer doing work on the highway. With a clear vision in mind, I assembled a team comprising a finance expert, a seasoned highway mowing specialist, a technician, a route strategist, and myself as the visionary.

In a remarkably short time, we pooled our talents and resources to craft a comprehensive bid, confident that we had all the necessary components to secure the project. Once again, I found myself at the helm of a new collaborative effort, driven by shared determination and purpose.

The level of intense scrutiny and barriers we encountered in breaking into this line of work took me by surprise. Despite my aversion to making excuses or placing blame when things did not go as planned, I found myself faced with the reality of our bid being rejected. Despite our meticulous preparation, thorough planning, and fervent prayers, the door was unceremoniously slammed shut in our faces. I must admit, I was devastated by the outcome. It was a bitter pill to swallow after investing so much time, effort, and hope into the endeavor. Yet, in the face of disappointment, I remained resolute in my determination to find another way forward.

After taking a deep breath, I reassured myself that the opportunity would resurface, and when it did, we would be ready. Unfortunately, the truth was that even upon its return, we would likely encounter the same outcome. Despite several attempts, it eventually became apparent that I would be the only one left standing. If you're reading this, I want to impart a guiding principle that has shaped my entire life—a simple yet powerful mantra: "Never Give Up!" Regardless of the obstacles you face, the opposition you encounter, your background, or perceived limitations, always remember that if you trust in God, He will provide everything you need, precisely when you need it.

I firmly believed that highway mowing, or as I knew it then, centerline mowing, would be a part of our true business calling. Even though we were consistently facing rejection, I was determined to uncover the reasons behind it. I knew I needed to address two key questions: 1) Why were we being denied? and 2) What steps could we take to overcome the obstacles blocking our path?

It became clear to me that the niche work we were pursuing demanded an exceptionally high level of safety standards. Entry into this field required rigorous adherence to safety protocols, and I realized that I needed to respond with the same level of diligence and commitment.

Hurricane Katrina

While pursuing my dreams and my desire to assist others, I felt drawn to the life-altering storm that wreaked havoc on Louisiana, Mississippi, and parts of Alabama. Once I made the decision to help, I turned to prayer and reached out to a few individuals. Before long, I had made connections and embarked on yet another piece of the puzzle. One of my objectives was to gain the necessary safety experience for the government contract by working alongside the road and clearing trees and debris. As the saying goes, "Man plans, and God laughs!"

Just about every possible challenge arose during this endeavor, but amidst the chaos, there were still silver linings. To begin with, I ventured into this undertaking with only a verbal agreement from an acquaintance of an acquaintance—no formal contract in place. As for accommodations, I found myself sleeping in my truck in the middle of Mississippi for about a month, relying on an onsite trailer to freshen up each morning. Despite these hurdles, there was no shortage of work available. Yet, we found ourselves positioned as a fourth-tier contractor, meaning the project passed through three intermediaries before reaching us—the ones carrying out the work.

Let me be clear—I willingly entered this arrangement fully aware of its implications. The fact that there were three entities receiving payment before the actual workers *(myself and our crew)* speaks volumes about the lucrative nature of the work. Despite the substantial income generated by the storm, there was a glaring issue with the setup. The individual scheduled to receive payment directly before me proved to be dishonest, causing significant challenges. Consequently, we found ourselves constantly chasing payments each week, often experiencing delays, or being shorted without any viable recourse other than resorting to violence—an option I refused to entertain.

Faced with the option to abandon my original purpose or adapt to the circumstances, I chose the latter—I was determined to acquire the necessary experience. Adopting a strategic approach, I shifted tactics and focused on building relationships. My first step was to obtain certification for flagging operations, positioning myself directly under a contractor. I reached out to a contractor involved in storm debris removal and negotiated a deal to work directly for them. We relocated closer to the city where our work was centered, securing hotel accommodations for the crew accompanying me, and immediately got to work.

I took the initiative to establish a rapport with the frontline supervisor from the Department of Forestry, confiding in him about the highs and lows of our experience—the funds invested, the payments withheld, and the purpose behind my efforts. For two to three months in Hattiesburg, Mississippi, we expended considerable resources. Amidst the challenges, we emerged with a recommendation letter that I believed held the potential to revolutionize my aspirations—to become a centerline mowing contractor.

Success is not merely a fleeting fantasy; it requires diligent effort and unwavering perseverance. The notion that one can simply dream of success and watch it effortlessly materialize is a fallacy. Achieving success demands hard work, determination, and resilience. At this juncture, I must pause and express my profound gratitude to my wife. Throughout our journey, she has been a pillar of support, patiently enduring my wild ideas, revelations, unconventional approaches, and occasional absence as we navigated both marriage and business together. Our shared experiences have led to many intense moments of fellowship, strengthening our bond as both spouses and partners in business.

Returning from our journey in Mississippi, I faced the stark reality of having expended well over $100k—funds we simply did not possess—on essential equipment such as dump trailers, chainsaws, hotel accommodations, dump fees, meals, and even a brand-new bobcat, mostly obtained through credit. To be candid, I was overcome with a sickening feeling in the pit of my stomach. In that moment of uncertainty, I once again turned to the source of my strength and sought guidance from God, questioning whether I had veered off course and deceived myself regarding my true calling. Yet, as always, His response echoed in my heart: "Trust Me."

With a renewed sense of resolve, I acknowledged my wounds, picked myself up, and returned to our office, ready to face the challenges ahead and resume our work. "How many 'no's will you accept before you believe that something is just not for you?" This question may puzzle many, but for me, the answer is elusive. Why? Because I am not wired to give up easily. My belief is simple: if God has spoken, His word is truth, unless He directs otherwise.

Before Hurricane Katrina and the notion of acquiring a Bobcat and a dump trailer, I had already recognized the necessity for a heavy duty truck larger than my Dodge Ram 1500, which was tasked with pulling a 7x14 enclosed trailer. Little did I know, this realization marked the inception of my venture into uncharted territory and would be exactly what I needed when the appropriate time came.

Grass Clips

Success often materializes when diligent preparation intersects with a timely opportunity.

It is ironic because being prepared doesn't ensure immediate success; it merely positions you to seize opportunities as they arise. Conversely, lacking readiness increases the likelihood of encountering failure, as you've mentally conceded defeat. Therefore, the key is to persevere and never give up.

One day, two of my close friends and business associates reached out and expressed their desire to visit New Orleans and witness the devastation firsthand. Sensing a need for a trip to decompress and reignite my vision in vibrant hues, I eagerly embraced the opportunity. Additionally, I had some outstanding funds to collect in Mississippi, making the timing ideal. We embarked on the journey along I-20, bound for New Orleans. During the drive, we engaged in lengthy prayer sessions, reflecting on life, contemplating the future, expressing concern for our loved ones, discussing potential opportunities ahead, and empathizing with all those affected by the hurricane.

At one point during the journey, I found myself praying fervently over the highway, reflecting on my aspirations of one day maintaining the grass along its sides. As we reached our first destination, the sight of the devastating aftermath left by Hurricane Katrina brought us to tears. Each of us was overcome with emotion, shedding tears like infants, enveloped in a somber mood. Despite the heart-wrenching scene before us, we continued to offer prayers for restoration, healing, and a miraculous turnaround for the city and its surrounding areas. We captured numerous photographs as mementos of our visit before continuing to Hattiesburg where I was slated to meet the individual with whom I had previously worked.

Upon arriving, we spotted him standing beside a gleaming brand-new candy apple red Corvette. Initially, a wave of resentment surged within me as I contemplated how I had been taken advantage of but as swiftly as the anger surfaced, it dissipated. Instead, I chose to approach him with a celebratory demeanor, complimenting his exquisite vehicle and inquiring about his well-being. In that moment, I realized a crucial lesson: my success would never be hindered by harboring resentment or jealousy towards someone else's achievements.

After exchanging pleasantries and expressing gratitude for the opportunity, I collected my final payment from him. With that concluded, we began our journey back to metro Atlanta. Throughout the return trip, we maintained our prayers and celebrations, reflecting on all the experiences we had encountered and all the blessings that lay ahead. It's worth noting that our prayers extended to encompass the lives of all those impacted by the storms, as we fervently asked for God's guidance in our present and future endeavors, desiring to be instrumental in bringing about positive solutions.

Ready, Set, Go!

Back in the saddle, I redirected my focus towards further developing the business. My confidence and determination were now even more resolute. Often, we perceive periods of adversity and setbacks through a negative lens, failing to recognize that each challenge is a vital piece of the puzzle leading to success. Without delay, I delved into strategizing how we could secure a highway contract. As the contracts came up for bid once again, having faced three previous unsuccessful attempts, the team working on this opportunity with us had significantly diminished. Only one individual remained beside me, and together, we collaborated on devising a plan to secure the contract.

Holding steadfast to the belief that true conviction knows no obstacles, I meticulously outlined my aspirations and fervently prayed for their realization. While prayer is undoubtedly powerful, I firmly believe in combining prayer with proactive effort rather than passively waiting for miracles to unfold. Hence, I wasted no time in reaching out to potential clients, specifically inquiring about their need for bush hogging services or any acquaintances with extensive overgrown properties. Serendipitously, an associate reached out, informing me of properties he had recently acquired that required bush hogging work.

It is imperative to grasp this crucial aspect: I hadn't previously divulged my intentions to him regarding pursuing this type of work. Yet, by putting my faith into tangible action, I witnessed immediate and concrete results. We promptly rented a tractor and proceeded to bush-hog several properties for his company. This opportunity served as the catalyst for yet another innovative idea. Fueled by firsthand experience and newfound momentum, I conceived the notion of approaching a municipality with an audacious proposal—to mow their roads for free, believe it or not. After all, who doesn't appreciate complimentary services? Remarkably, they expressed keen interest and graciously welcomed us to their planning office, providing us with a comprehensive tour, maps, and even allowing us to shadow one of their crews to observe their day-to-day operations.

With a meticulously crafted plan in hand, we set out on a designated day to survey the roads ripe for mowing in the

County. Anticipation hung thick in the air as we envisioned acquiring the vital experience and skills needed for our venture. As we approached a four-way stop sign enroute, I cast a fleeting glance to the right, only to spot a car mere feet away from the passenger side of the truck where I sat. In the blink of an eye, the crash happened, and just like that, the momentum of our business endeavor was altered.

Thankfully, neither of us sustained injuries in the accident, but the driver of the other vehicle was not as fortunate. Sadly, the collision resulted in the total loss of my last remaining partner's truck. In the immediate aftermath, I swiftly dialed my wife's number, urgently requesting her to bring water to the scene for the injured gentleman while we awaited an ambulance. In the wake of the incident, my partner made the difficult decision to move on, leaving me to grapple with the shattered remnants of "my dream".

This moment crystallized a profound truth within me: a genuine dream is one that you're willing to pursue, even if it means standing alone in its pursuit. It underscored the stark difference between mere speculation and a true dream—one that demands unwavering commitment and resilience, even in the face of adversity.

Keep Dreaming!

Seated by the window of my beloved Waffle House, a sanctuary of comfort, with the morning newspaper in hand and a sumptuous breakfast before me, I carved out a sacred space for reflection. Lost in the rhythm of sizzling bacon and steaming coffee, I allowed my mind to wander freely, indulging in daydreams and visions inspired by divine guidance. With each bite, I savored the flavors of gratitude for past blessings and anticipation for the future's untold adventures.

Outside the window, the bustling highways of Rockdale County, Georgia, hummed with activity as tractors and trucks forged their paths. Inspired by the industrious spirit of my surroundings, I felt a stirring within, a renewed belief in our boundless potential and the power of faith to propel us forward. Fueled by this conviction, I resolved to embark on a new journey, to transcend the confines of familiarity.

With determination coursing through my veins, I set forth to our local John Deere dealership, ready to transform my vision into reality. After engaging in conversations with the sales agent, I made the bold decision to fill out a credit application for some tractors. The sales agent's question about the start date of our contract caught me off guard. With a hint of skepticism in his eyes, he asked, "When does your contract begin?"

I could sense his surprise when I responded that we didn't have one yet. It was a moment where the raised eyebrows and side glances spoke volumes to those who doubted what I already knew deep within.

Undeterred, I explained to him our approach of proactive preparation for what I firmly believed was on the horizon. Embracing a mindset of anticipation, I began sharing my unconventional plan with others: acquiring tractors and initiating highway cutting without a formal agreement in place. It may have sounded absurd to some, but I was determined to forge ahead with unwavering confidence.

In response to inquiries about our identity and legitimacy, I confidently stated that we would produce video evidence of our work performed, a testament to our capabilities and commitment. It was a bold step into the unknown, fueled by faith and a steadfast belief in the vision that lay before us.

Grass Clips

If you truly believe in your dreams,
you must be prepared to sound a bit unconventional
at times, even if it means appearing
out of touch with reality.

My words seemed to resonate with the sales agent. He extended a generous invitation for my mentor and I to tour one of John Deere's plants in North Carolina. To my astonishment, they even arranged for us to visit a facility where tractors were manufactured. It was a testament to the power of dreaming big! With each invitation, I sensed myself drawing closer to the fulfillment of God's promises in breaking into this new line of business. I owe immense gratitude to my wife, Shawn, for her unwavering belief and support amidst my most audacious pursuits and dreams.

Amidst the hustle and bustle of our office, my wife, Shawn, carved out a special play area for our son Justin, ensuring he was cared for while I pursued my dreams. She tirelessly handled all the back-office tasks that enabled me to focus on envisioning the future. Despite the demands of our growing business, we remained steadfast in our efforts, dispatching our three trucks each day. My days were filled with overseeing operations on job sites ensuring our work lived up to our slogan, "We Manicure Lawns." I refused to sit idly by without acting.

Driven by a relentless determination, I sought opportunities to expand our reach. In my quest for answers, I contacted an expert in securing contracts for highway *(referred to as centerline)* mowing. With a specific question burning in my mind, I inquired about our inability to secure a contract. His response was simple yet profound: we needed both experience and favor on our side.

With this newfound clarity, I redoubled our efforts, determined to acquire the necessary experience, and cultivate favor to propel us toward our goals. In response, I stated that we already possessed favor and questioned how we were expected to gain experience if we were never given a chance to prove ourselves. His silence spoke volumes, leaving me with no further insight. Yet, far from deterred, I hung up the phone.

Chapter Five

MORE GRASS,
MORE PROBLEMS

Highway Mowing

*P*eriodically, the John Deere sales agent would reach out for updates, and vice versa. Though the timing was uncertain, I held steadfast faith that our breakthrough would come. Then, while servicing a client, my phone rang—it was my wife, Shawn. With anticipation, I answered, and she delivered surprising but expected news. "We received a call from a company handling centerline mowing on a major highway," she said. "They're interested in subcontracting with us."

Overflowing with gratitude, I immediately lifted praises to God, and Shawn joined in, acknowledging His hand in all things. Finally, the moment had arrived, and I eagerly sought details about the conversation. Inquiring about the origin of their contact, the timeline for commencement, the required equipment, and the scope of work, we decided to convene and draft specific questions. Upon reconnecting with the company, we expressed our enthusiasm and gratitude for the opportunity, while also seeking answers to our questions. With preparations underway, we learned we had just 10 business days to mobilize—a tight time frame due to the company's imminent risk of contract default. The realization hit me like a tidal wave, leaving me brimming with excitement and my mind abuzz with plans for the next steps.

Having a dream or vision is one thing but living it in real-time can be daunting. Here we were, faced with a "put up or shut up" moment, lacking tractors, employees, experience, or financing to seize this opportunity. Yet, what we lacked in resources, we made up for with sheer determination and faith to press onward. After a swift strategy session, I made my next call to the tractor dealership with a simple declaration: "It is time!" I'm certain they never expected such a call, let alone the urgency with which we needed them to act.

With just ten days to fully operationalize this complex new venture, we dove headfirst into the process. Once the paperwork was signed and set in motion, I consulted my checklist, bracing myself for the multitude of tasks ahead. We required six tractors and bush hogs, along with twenty-five weed trimmers, blowers, safety signs, dump trailers, and trucks. The magnitude of these moving parts was not lost on me, particularly given our precarious financial situation. Leveraging every ounce of available credit, we scrambled to piece together the necessary resources.

As the deadline drew near, and with only one week left before our scheduled start date, a significant obstacle presented itself: we had no employees. In a moment of quick thinking, we hastily created flyers, distributed them to local businesses, and placed an ad in a major metro Atlanta newspaper. I couldn't help but wonder if there were tractor drivers in a bustling city like Atlanta. With a heavy heart, I closed my eyes, a solitary tear escaping and tracing a path down my cheek, as doubts crept in. Was I truly following God's guidance, or was I merely pursuing my desires, lost in familiar doubts and uncertainties?

Grass Clips

While chasing your dreams, expect setbacks and dark days that challenge your resolve.

With just a few days left before beginning the contract, I remained confident that everything would fall into place for the company. Fortunately, I had secured a transport company to move our new tractors. Miraculously, we received exactly four responses to our tractor driver ad in the newspaper, and we hired all four applicants. Additionally, two individuals currently working with us claimed to have experience, including one who served as our maintenance supervisor at the time.

We were fortunate that John Deere offered a large tract of land and agreed to facilitate a two-day training course for our drivers. Later we discovered, that driving a tractor on a farm versus navigating it on the side of the road with tractor-trailers and cars whizzing by on the interstate would prove to be a stark contrast. This lack of experience soon became an ongoing challenge for our venture.

During the two-day training sessions, I believe we fostered strong camaraderie and provided comprehensive training but due to my other responsibilities, I couldn't be present for most of the training. To address this, I hired someone to serve as a working supervisor to handle fieldwork issues in my absence. Surveying the scene, it seemed we had most of the necessary components in place—a truly miraculous feat. While we still lacked all the on-ground workers, I remained confident that we could secure assistance closer to the job location.

Grass Clips

If you wait for everything to be perfect before pursuing your dream, you might find yourself nearing the end of your days still waiting. Walking and working in faith always leads to the next step of the journey toward your dream.

As the agreed-upon start time rapidly approached, I reached out to our transport company to confirm their readiness to move our equipment approximately two and a half hours from our location toward the bordering state. To my dismay, the response I received was unexpected: they were unable to transport the six tractors and bush hogs for us.

Facing a financial crunch, we could not afford to pay the exorbitant rates for the quick transport of so many units. With no one to confide in and hesitant to burden my supportive wife, I turned to the one source I knew I could always count on, my

Father in Heaven. His advice was clear: think outside the box. Doubts and concerns flooded my mind—"We can't do that," "It's insane," "What if we get pulled over by the police?"—I uttered aloud, "Let's just drive them a couple of hundred miles on the highway!" It seemed audacious, even reckless, but as the idea took shape, I couldn't help but wonder: Would we dare to take such a risk?

When life responds with 'NO,' God's answer is 'YES.' This became my mantra. I rallied our drivers for an impromptu Sunday morning field trip, preparing for work to commence the following day. Calling upon one of my closest friends from The Network, I set the plan into motion. Departing at daybreak, we navigated the highways with six tractors flanked by trucks equipped with flashing lights, creating the illusion of a legitimate operation. After an eight-hour journey, punctuated by a breakfast stop at IHOP, we arrived at our destination. This bold endeavor underscored a simple truth: bold steps are necessary when expecting bold results.

Upon receiving the contract, I discovered a stipulation: the on-site supervisor couldn't participate in the mowing crew and was limited to a strictly supervisory role. Adhering to the rules, I recognized the urgent need for action, prompting me to assume dual roles as both supervisor and fixer. To adapt, I devised a strategy: I started my day in khakis and a polo shirt, keeping work clothes and boots in my vehicle alongside baby wipes for quick freshening up when necessary. Success, I realized, never arrives without resilience, even in moments of weakness and despair. After mowing the highway grass for about two months and finally finding our footing, an unexpected call arrived.

"Mr. Steve, we need you right now, and it's not good," came the urgent plea from the other end of the phone call. Without knowing the exact issue, I summoned my calm and reverted into supervisor mode. Before the call, I had been weed-trimming areas of concern highlighted by the inspector. Working diligently alone, far behind the crew, I ensured that we would pass inspection and could bill for the work completed. Now, it was time to take charge. In a daze, I embarked on the ride to the location of the issue, enveloped in an uneasy silence punctuated only by the sounds of the open road, praying for guidance every step of the way.

As I arrived at the scene, a sense of urgency permeated the air, with numerous individuals in safety vests and firetrucks with EMTs milling around, deliberating their next course of action. Amidst the chaos, a heart-wrenching cry echoed through the air, piercing the silence. Driven by a mix of curiosity and concern, I approached cautiously, only to be met with a sight that would haunt and amaze me for years to come.

One of our tractors lay on its side, its massive frame dwarfing the figure trapped beneath. Frantically, their hands moved up and down, a desperate plea for help. The tractor, navigating an incline, had struck a hidden hole concealed by the tall grass, causing it to overturn, pinning the operator's leg beneath its weight.

The Power of Prayer

At that moment, hearing the anguished cries of the tractor driver, the very foundation of our new venture seemed to crumble. It felt like a futile and unnecessary risk. Yet, with the steadfast composure of a man of faith, I held onto the belief that this challenge was just another opportunity to showcase our resilience and determination.

Grass Clips

When tough times roll in,
will you lay down and allow them to
run over you, or will you muster all your
strength and face them head-on?
Faith never quits!

Each morning, before our crews set off to work, I made it a point to gather everyone for a motivational reading followed by prayer. Together, we prayed for safety and a spirit of excellence in all our endeavors for the day. Participation was never mandatory, and I made sure everyone on the team knew they were free to choose whether to join in the prayer.

Our weed-trimming supervisor consistently opted out of our daily prayers, choosing instead to stand on the sidelines. Despite this, I never asked why and made a point not to treat him any differently. I continued to encourage and support him just like everyone else on the team. As I stood there, scanning the scene, and feeling almost helpless, I remembered my identity in Christ and summoned all the guys to circle up and join hands. To my surprise, the very first person to grab my hand was the same individual who always opted out of our prayers.

To this day, all I can impart to those who will read this book is the importance of never judging others and always showing respect, even when you perceive that others may not support or share your beliefs. In that pivotal moment, I reached out and clasped his hand, exchanging a brief smile and a nod of mutual respect. Together, we prayed fervently for a miracle. It felt like hours passed as we continued to lift our voices in prayer until finally, the firefighters and EMT workers found a way to free the trapped driver from beneath the weight of the tractor.

They deployed specialized blow-up bags to gradually lift and stabilize sections of the tractor, carefully maneuvering to avoid any sudden movements that could worsen the situation. Due to the precarious position of the tractor on a slope, the process stretched out over several hours, with every move calculated to prevent further harm to the trapped operator.

When they finally succeeded in freeing him, a Life Flight helicopter landed on the interstate. The scene was eerily quiet, with no traffic moving and not a single vehicle in sight, as if time stood still amid the tense rescue operation.

Grass Clips

What may seem like the darkest hours of life often becomes God's playground for miracles.

As they carefully moved the tractor driver onto a gurney, my attention was drawn to a group of people on the overpass, holding hands in a display of unity. Their presence struck me as if they understood the power of connection. As the paramedics approached the helicopter, I found myself drawn to them, and in a moment of awe, I witnessed what seemed to be crushed bones in the driver's ankle reshaping back into form. Lost in the miraculous sight, I was startled by someone telling me I was not allowed ride in the helicopter. Instead, law enforcement permitted me to drive traffic-free to the nearest hospital, which was over thirty minutes away. With prayers on my lips, I quickly jumped into my truck and sped towards the hospital.

I have no recollection of the drive, except for arriving and walking into the hospital. After checking in at the front desk, I was instructed to wait for a doctor to provide an update. Eventually, the doctor emerged and inquired if I was with the gentleman involved in the tractor rollover. I confirmed, likely evident by my safety vest matching his attire. With a stunned expression, the doctor led me to the X-ray area, where he showed me a chart and asked if I was certain this was the individual from the accident. I affirmed, and he pointed to the X-ray, revealing that aside from some scratches, there was not a single broken bone or severe damage. Remarkably, the tractor driver could be back at work the very next day.

The following day, I rode to meet several crews at a gas station. My mind couldn't help but reflect on the events that happened less than twenty-four hours ago when I uttered, "It is over." I believed there was no way out of our predicament. Indeed, we encountered numerous challenges during this project. On the very first day of the contract, one of our tractor drivers overturned a unit in a small ditch, crushing the cab and rendering it inoperable. Despite this setback, I remained determined to find a silver lining. I swiftly reassigned another one of our drivers to a different team until we could get the tractor repaired.

Unbeknownst to me, our tractor insurance wouldn't take effect until the next day, leaving us to foot the bill for repairs out of a pocket already stretched thin. To make matters worse, it took us nearly two weeks to mow less than a mile of highway, a completely unacceptable pace. At this point, you might be thinking, "If these guys didn't have bad luck, they'd have no luck at all!" Despite the setbacks, we pressed on. When one of my team members narrowly avoided being mauled by the tractor, a barrage of questions flooded my mind: Is this too much? Am I out of my league? Did I truly hear from God? How will I face my wife with this failure? These rapid-fire inquiries weighed heavily on my conscience.

In the early 2000s, a popular TV game show called "Who Wants to be a Millionaire?" captivated audiences, offering contestants the chance to win big prizes. Intrigued by the possibility of someone winning the jackpot, I occasionally tuned in. One of the rules allowed contestants to "Phone a Friend" when they encountered a difficult question with the caveat being they only had one lifeline. When we place our trust in God, He is far more generous than any game show. He provides us with multiple opportunities to call on Him, often placing people in our lives to fulfill specific spiritual roles.

I dialed the phone and reached out to none other than the $39.99 Lawn Care Guy, my mentor. I started to express, "It's over," but he promptly interrupted, reminding me of my identity in Christ. As doubts crept in, my faith surged, and I began to affirm, "Father, I trust You. Father, I trust You!" He prayed for me without prior knowledge of the situation.

Later, I encountered several individuals who prayed for me, despite not knowing the specifics of what had occurred.

Grass Clips

When giving up is not an option, give in to
the only option for success: Christ.

When I arrived at the gas station, seeking respite from the sweltering heat, I ventured inside to grab a drink. As I stood in line, a woman's gaze lingered on me, prompting a moment of discomfort. Hoping to avoid any awkwardness, I averted my eyes, but she approached me before I left the store. "Were you with the guys involved in the accident on the highway yesterday?" she inquired. Confirming her suspicion, I nodded. Locking eyes with me, she solemnly stated, "I was with the group on top of the bridge, praying as you guys prayed." In an instant, we shared a smile, united by our faith during that pivotal moment.

She then inquired about the worker's condition, and with the widest smile I could muster, I shared that he was back to work already! Joy filled the air as we celebrated this miraculous turn-around right there in the store. It was a reminder that God will rescue any of us in our time of need; we just need to be willing to embark on the journey He has planned for us. In that moment, it didn't matter who we were or where we came from—our backgrounds, financial statuses—all that mattered was that we joined hand in hand, praying, and our spirits connected!

With my faith soaring to new heights, I dove into action with unwavering determination, completing tasks at breakneck speed. Each day, I trailed behind the trimming crew, meticulously tidying up the areas they overlooked. You might wonder why I didn't just have them redo their work. Well, I saw this as an opportunity to deepen my appreciation for the effort put in by the team. By tackling these tasks myself, I gained invaluable insights into our workflow and identified areas for improvement. I believed this approach would streamline our operations, expedite billing, and maintain cash flow—or so I thought.

Despite the setback of losing two tractors due to accidents, our determination remained unwavering. Grassman, a close friend who joined us as a field supervisor, proved to be an invaluable asset with his mechanical expertise. After the initial tractor mishap, I connected with a skilled individual at the John Deere shop who assisted in repairing the damages—a meeting for which I am eternally grateful. The intensity of our efforts took a toll on me physically, evident when one of my worn-out boots fell apart while trimming one day. I found myself navigating the roadside debris by hopping on one leg to avoid injury as I made my way back to the truck.

As we moved forward with our work, it felt like the highway stretched endlessly. Yet, despite the challenges, we eventually completed the second part of our task. With four different sections of highway to cut, the last one necessitated transporting the tractors by truck. To optimize our operations, I notified the apartment complex that had generously accommodated us on a month-to-month rental basis that we would be vacating due to our change in work location.

After everyone packed up their belongings, I stayed an extra day to meticulously clean each apartment, ensuring they were returned in better condition than when we received them. As I deflated my air mattress, neatly folded it, and gathered my belongings to load into the truck, I passed through the kitchen and noticed a note attached to the refrigerator. Drawing closer, I realized it was a quote, one I had committed to memory after reading it every morning from John Maxwell's *21 Irrefutable Laws of Leadership*. The quote read, "If you do the things, you ought to do when you ought to do them, then you can do the things you want to do when you want to do them. Hard work is just an accumulation of easy things gone undone." Those words served as a daily reminder, motivating me to address the small tasks promptly, knowing they could prevent larger issues down the road. I soon learned that merely acknowledging it wasn't enough; action was required. With each experience, we gained valuable insight, propelling us forward to the next location.

Grass Clips

Every stride toward success, regardless of its size or the effort it demands, merits celebration and applause.

At the next location, we had to complete a stretch of highway less than twenty-five miles long. I anticipated us only being there a short while, so we hit the ground running. Everything seemed to be going well until one morning as we were getting ready to start our day, I received a phone call to meet one of our crews where a tractor was located. I asked what the problem was and was told someone had tampered with the tractor. I thought to myself okay maybe someone tried to flatten a tire or siphon gas and finally landed on it can't be too bad.

As I arrived, I noticed the hood of the tractor was up, and some of the crew members were shaking their heads. The sight of all the electrical lines pulled out of the tractor nearly paralyzed me with frustration. Yet, refusing to succumb to negativity, I rallied the team to action. With determination in my heart, I called the local John Deere dealer for repairs and swiftly shifted focus back to the task at hand. No setback would deter us. Each day, we pressed forward with unwavering resolve, inching closer to our goal.

Grass Clips

To have success in anything, you must be willing to accept the help of others and humble yourself to listen to sound advice.

Gains and Losses

Whenever we found ourselves overwhelmed with trimming and litter control, my mentor, the $39.99 Lawn Care Guy, came to our aid. It was a true blessing, as he never expected payment or anything in return. Observing his actions, I learned valuable lessons in leadership. Whenever he visited, he'd arrive loaded with snacks, ice-cold water, and drinks. But what truly set him apart was his personal touch. He would visit each worker to distribute refreshments with care and gratitude. What struck me was the care and thoughtfulness with which he treated each worker. As they enjoyed the snacks, he provided a trash bag for wrappers. Then, with the water bottles, he'd ask each person to hold out their arms, pouring water over their wrists to cool them down in the Georgia heat. It was a simple gesture, but it revitalized the crew, boosting morale and productivity. It was a reminder that we all need someone in our corner to help us turn the corner towards improvement.

Once, my wife spent the entire night in tears after learning from the prime contractor how we were expected to maneuver the tractors across the highway to reach the median areas for mowing. Their response was as stark as it was daunting: "You kind of have to play Chicken or Frogger, hit the gas, and don't look back. Then pray you get to the median." Picture this: a slow-moving tractor amidst the rush of cars and trucks on the Interstate Highway System.

The nerves and sheer audacity required by the operator to attempt such a feat are beyond imagination. That was the reality we faced daily as we tackled our task despite vehicles speeding by at 65 to 85 miles per hour. Often, the rush of passing vehicles was the only breeze and respite from the heat we experienced. Yet, we considered each day that we returned to our rooms safely as a glorious and immensely successful day.

One day, as we were about to wrap up our work for the day, the rush hour traffic started to intensify. Typically, this stretch of highway flowed smoothly, unlike the congested city areas. This time, in a surreal moment, a vehicle soared over our heads. It was a shocking scene: an accident occurred, causing a normal vehicle on the highway to become airborne, directly above us, before crashing down partially onto one of our vehicles. Our team reacted with screams, frantic movements, and desperate attempts to seek cover.

Miraculously, there were no major injuries or significant damage to our vehicle despite its poor condition after the collision. Still reeling from the shock, I quickly gathered everyone together to ensure no one had been harmed by the flying glass or debris. Thankfully, everyone was physically unharmed, but the ordeal was far from over. When the police arrived, they requested each member's driver's license and insurance information due to the damage sustained by our vehicle.

As luck would have it, our driver turned out to have an outstanding warrant, unbeknownst to us, and was promptly handcuffed and taken to the local jail. Murphy's law seemed to be in full effect –anything that could go wrong went wrong. Losing our main supervisor for trimming and litter pickup was a significant setback, given his bilingual skills and organizational role within our ground crews. After ensuring everyone was safe and out of the median, we called it a day and I headed to the jail to check on our supervisor. Following the necessary procedures, we managed to bail him out several days later.

Despite this setback, we completed our tasks in the area without further incident and prepared for the final leg of our journey in centerline mowing.

Things appeared to be improving with only occasional

breakdowns and minor issues. To facilitate our operations for the final part of our initial mowing cycle, I arranged extended-stay lodging for myself. The plan was to mow each highway three times throughout the season. This area, closer to our home base, allowed most of the team to return home each evening and resume work the next day. Little did I know, this phase would prove to be the most pivotal for both the company and me personally, but not for the reasons you might expect.

The challenges continued to pile up during this phase. First, we faced a punctured gas tank, which required a makeshift repair in the field, thanks to Grassman's mechanical skills. Then, our tires began going flat, necessitating costly repairs that strained our already dwindling funds. Just when it seemed things couldn't get any worse, our entire ground crew walked off the job, leaving us scrambling to bring in additional lawn maintenance crews to pick up the slack. This unexpected expense forced us to pay out hefty overtime wages, further draining our financial resources.

It was a tough blow when we received the call informing us that we were being replaced, bringing our highway mowing venture to an abrupt end. I faced the difficult task of letting go of our crews, and I had to deliver this short letter to each of them: "We regret to inform you that we will no longer be performing work on the highway. Today will be your last day of employment with us. We want to express our sincere appreciation for your hard work and dedication during this venture. We wish you all the best in your future endeavors."

There was a mixed reaction among our team members when they received the news. Sadly, I lost one of my closest friends,

The Grassman, that day, along with a few other relationships, and that's something I deeply regret. Even amid failure, it's crucial to navigate with dignity and respect, striving to minimize the pain for all involved. Despite my efforts, I recognize I fell short in some respects. All I could do was hope that our recovery would overshadow the setback we faced.

I must confess that despite my concern for our employees, a significant part of me felt relieved. Finally, I could breathe without the weight of constant scrutiny and pressure. I welcomed the opportunity for a break and some much-needed rest. The timing, in fact, seemed almost impeccable, considering the ongoing issues we were facing.

Lawyers and Equipment

While the venture had come to an end for everyone else, it hadn't reached its complete conclusion for me. There were still loose ends to tie up. Our tractors were scattered across various locations each bearing the scars of our inexperience and the rough terrain. Retrieving them for repossession meant parking my truck and driving each tractor to the dealership, then walking back to my truck—or, in a few instances, catching a ride back.

With some of the tractors disconnected from their mowers, I had to hook them up to the back of my truck and transport them separately, navigating the interstate at a sluggish 20- to 25-miles per hour. Amidst the cacophony of people shouting all sorts of things at a man already feeling rattled and disappointed, I steadfastly kept my windows rolled up, focusing solely on what lay ahead and the task at hand.

After relocating all the tractors except for the one involved in the accident, I received an urgent notice from an inspector demanding immediate removal. Fearing repercussions, I turned to a friend who previously assisted us with tractor repairs. Graciously, he agreed to help again, and together, in the dead of night, we spent 4 to 5 hours towing the tractor and mower back to the dealership with our vehicles. As we completed the task, a sigh of relief escaped me, and I felt a weight lift off my shoulders.

Grass Clips

Success often resembles a glamor shot,
where imperfections are airbrushed away, and only
the best light and angles are showcased.
But how many are willing to lift the veil and reveal the
authentic picture? It's not always pretty, but it's
a glimpse of the real you, just like success.

The equipment was retrieved from the highway and safely stored at the dealership, but this was only the start of our challenges. During the deposition that would soon come, lawyers on one side of the table bombarded me with questions regarding the non-payment of the equipment we obtained. I listed all the reasons why we hadn't fulfilled our financial obligations and ultimately had the tractors repossessed. Throughout my life, I've always placed great importance on the integrity of my word in any financial dealings conducted in my name. Thus, sitting there and having to justify my failure was a heavy burden to bear.

Despite facing immense pressure and being pursued by the credit company for over $500K we managed to negotiate a settlement for $50K. While some may not see this as a cause for celebration, I wholeheartedly disagree. It's not about the amount paid, but about my faith and resolve. During the ordeal, our lawyer commended me for handling the intense questioning with the poise of a seasoned veteran. He framed the $50K settlement as a down payment for the invaluable education we gained from this experience. With that perspective, I knew without a doubt that somehow, someway, we would rise again. Reality set in as I got into my vehicle, wondering where in the world we would come up with the money to pay that 50K settlement!

Grass Clips

When you're willing to release your worries to God,
You realize that the very thing you are worried
about has no power over you at all.

Not more than a few weeks after the deposition, I was driving down the Interstate when something caught my eye: two of our new vehicles being towed on a wrecker truck. I blinked in disbelief, wondering if I was dreaming or lost in some sort of fog. I turned my vehicle around and hurried back to the office. To my dismay, my eyes hadn't deceived me. The trucks had indeed been repossessed.

As I sank back into my desk chair, I drew in a deep breath and uttered, "God, your will be done," my voice barely above a whisper. Tears streamed down my cheeks as I grappled with what felt like an avalanche of failures. Yet, amid my despair, a newfound strength and determination surged within me. Rising from my seat, I reminded myself of my identity in Christ. With resolve, I wiped away my tears and declared, "If God be for me, then who can be against me?" And just like that, I found myself back in strategizing mode. While I had no clue what the future held after these unfortunate events, I couldn't shake the sense that somehow, everything would eventually be alright.

Chapter Six

AN INVITE TO GROWTH

The Million Dollar Invite

hortly after, we found ourselves landing additional commercial contracts and building a solid roster of valued clients. With three commercial trucks in operation and a spare truck and trailer on standby, we were well-equipped to handle any overflow. As the business expanded, my focus shifted towards maintaining consistency and honing my skills as a business leader. During this time, an intriguing opportunity arose through one of my contacts: an invitation to attend a private meeting with a group of businessmen.

The invitation came with a stipulation: attendees were required to be running a minimum million-dollar-a-year business—an achievement we had not yet reached. Perplexed, I questioned my contact about why he extended the invitation despite our inability to meet the criteria. His response was a vote of confidence that echoed in my mind long after our conversation ended. "Steve," he said, "of all the people I know in this industry, I believe you will get there and prevail over any challenges." His words left me both humbled and inspired, but also added a new layer of pressure to our journey.

The meeting was nothing short of inspiring, one moment stood out and stayed with me long after it ended. A gentleman shared that the most important part of his day was when he did absolutely nothing. Intrigued, I leaned in to hear more. He explained that during this time, he cut off all forms of communication and simply focused on the goodness of God and the countless blessings in his life. It was a time to listen to God's voice and express gratitude for His presence.

This revelation sparked a revolution in my relationship with God and reshaped my focus on what He desires from me. It taught me the value of stillness and the profound impact it can have on our spiritual journey. Amidst the rush of passing vehicles and the fragrance of blooming trees, I found solace on a weathered bench, allowing myself to be enveloped in contemplation. Despite the ongoing challenges and setbacks, I made a conscious decision to document every trial, along with the lessons learned and strategies devised for overcoming them. During that tumultuous first highway venture, I kept a small notepad tucked within my safety vest, ready to capture any insights that crossed my mind. It became a repository of wisdom, a reservoir of foresight to guide me through future endeavors.

Grass Clips

Preparation starts the moment you believe.
It's not a destination but a continuous journey.
Ready yourself from the outset.

Despite the previous failure, I meticulously documented every detail of the previous contract, from team members to equipment setup. I mapped out strategies to maximize efficiency and results. Quitting wasn't an option for the little boy from Little River, South Carolina, who once stared at maggots at the bottom of an outhouse while being ridiculed.

On my way to Indiana to visit my oldest son, the phone rang, and it was my trusted business partner and faithful wife, Shawn, with the kind of excitement in her voice that you always remember. "We won, we won, we won!" Several months after the first centerline mowing venture had failed, for reasons unknown, the state put all the mowing contracts back up for bid. Armed with experience and a better understanding of their requirements, we bid for the most challenging area. Some might call it insane to try a more difficult area after failing at a less challenging one. In this area, travel wasn't necessary, and we had strong relationships close to our home base. Though excited, I remained cautious, knowing not to count any chickens before they hatched. With my notes in hand, we immediately praised God, and I spent the rest of the journey making mental preparations for what lay ahead.

It was quite the journey to muster the courage and pursue bids once more. We oscillated between yes and no, with my business partner firmly against the idea of submitting a bid. Her concerns were valid, and I couldn't offer many compelling reasons why she should trust me and try again. Indeed, one of the most crucial elements of a marriage is when a wife trusts the presence of God within her husband more than she trusts the man himself and yields to God's guidance. I prayed earnestly, asking for God's intervention to bring us to a consensus on moving forward. I firmly believed that if we couldn't find alignment in our decisions, success would remain elusive.

It may sound improbable, but the breakthrough came through an unexpected source—her hairdresser, a man, who asked her if she trusted the God within me for the decisions that needed to be made. When she came home and said, "Honey, I trust you and know that God will cover us," it was a profound moment. As I drove, I reflected on the journey, from disappointments to the joy of perseverance, and couldn't help but chuckle at the irony. Several weeks later, we received the official notice that we were indeed the awarded vendor for the contract, right in our backyard, and the largest and most challenging in the state!

The first thing this opportunity demanded was double the tractors and triple the personnel, trucks, and small handheld equipment. This was crucial due to the area's high traffic volume, a constant bottleneck throughout the day. After expressing gratitude to God for His blessings, my immediate concern was securing the tractors, especially after recent repossessions. You might wonder how I believed we could manage, especially now that we needed twelve! Despite financial constraints, faith and creativity would bridge the gaps. I reached out to my trusted mentor, the $39.99 Lawn Care Guy, and arranged a meeting to share the exciting news and discuss a proposed plan of action.

Grass Clips

When people go out of their way to help you,
it is essential to reciprocate and bless them
when your situation improves.

We went on to purchase the tractors. "I don't think I've ever had anyone be that detailed about ordering a tractor before," he remarked. Those little notebooks I mentioned earlier, where I diligently recorded my thoughts on the side of the highway, were proving to be invaluable. I had meticulously detailed and laid out specific specifications for each tractor, from the tires to the cab configuration.

We needed heavy duty tires that didn't require filling with antifreeze and water. The tires had to be flipped to provide a wider stance for the tractors. We opted against cab tractors due to their tendency to become top-heavy, among other issues. This wider stance would prevent the tractors from flipping over, while the specially foamed-filled tires would minimize costly repairs and downtime. As I confidently outlined these specifications, I momentarily forgot the hefty price tag and the blemish of repossession on my credit.

Undeterred, I brushed aside any concerns about cost and confidently moved forward. Besides, we decided to split the contract with the $39.99 Lawn Care Guy, which would help offset some of the expenses. When the sales team presented the final numbers, I maintained my composure outwardly, despite inwardly flinching. "Sounds good, let's get it done!" I exclaimed. At that moment, we were poised to become their largest customer, completely unaware of the recent challenges we had overcome.

Grass Clips

Never underestimate the power of
confidence and timing. When they align,
an unstoppable force is born.

The sales team returned with promising news: "Mr. Bromell, it will take about eight weeks, and we should have everything you requested ready to go." Look at God! If you don't believe yet, just keep reading. And if you do believe in the power of faith, keep reading!

The Previous Contractor

During our preparations, I received a letter that I could hardly believe. We were being dragged into court over the contract we just received. Don't ask me why, but after the initial shock, I smiled and said, "No weapon formed against me shall prosper," and I knew without a doubt it was our time to shine. We had no money for legal representation, so I decided to simply show up to court and see what happens.

The plaintiff, who was the previous contractor, held the contract for many years prior. He was highly regarded as the only company capable of handling the difficult task of mowing the metro area with all its dangers and terrain. He contended that we lacked the necessary experience and professionalism to complete the job and staunchly believed that the contract rightfully belonged to his company.

His company was represented by a couple of lawyers and had written depositions from the company we subcontracted with previously. The lawyers had a lot to say, as they were trying to drag us through the mud. I was told I didn't need to be on the stand; the entity that awarded the contracts would provide representation. As I sat in the back of the courtroom, the lawyers sparred before the judge. On day two, the judge interrupted, asking a simple question.

"As I rode into the courtroom today, I noticed the grass being cut on the side of the road. Is that so?" inquired the judge.

"Yes, Your Honor," replied the defense.

The judge continued, "Who is currently doing the work?"

With a slight grin and confidence, the response came, "BML, Inc., our company."

"And they are doing a fantastic job!" added the judge.

With that, the session concluded, the case was dismissed, and we were moving forward.

Grass Clips

Indeed, whatever God has destined for you is yours,
and nothing anyone says or does can thwart it.

Have you ever longed for something so deeply, only to face relentless obstacles just when it seemed within reach? It felt like finally stepping into the rainbow's embrace, inching closer to that elusive pot of gold. For me, that treasure wasn't merely about wealth or possessions; it symbolized holding my head high, recalling the little boy peering over the outhouse, confronting maggots, and discovering resilience amidst adversity.

We had the tractors prepared and made calls to secure trimmers, trucks, and all the necessary safety gear. Next, we needed over 100 people and drivers. Most of the individuals we worked with previously were reluctant to engage in highway work, except for one individual who had prior experience with us and was still part of our commercial mowing department. As my phone buzzed incessantly, I answered and was summoned to a meeting on the side of the highway, of all places.

I contacted the trusted team, including the $39.99 Lawn Care Guy and another individual from The Network, to join me for the meeting. Unsure of what to expect, I prepared myself for anything as we arrived at the location. Stepping out of our truck and activating our safety lights, we were greeted by several older gentlemen. One of them, who appeared to be in charge, approached me and inquired about Mr. Steve. Instantly, I felt a sense of respect for him.

Often, we fail to give each other the benefit of the doubt, assuming we'll wrong each other somehow. I soon discovered the older gentleman had good intentions; he and the others approached me as if they knew I was a businessman. The other gentleman was a jolly, large guy with a hearty laugh, and he shook my hand, remarking, "I did not know you were so young; you are not what we were expecting." After introductions were made, what followed set the course for future success. The man seemingly in charge said, "If you will have us, we will work as hard as you have ever seen a group of people work for the success of any venture." What caught my attention was the "us" part. So, I looked around and paused, then asked, "Who is us?" He grinned ever so slightly, replying, "We have enough guys to do the entire contract, and we will call you to meet the rest of our team."

On the way to that meeting, memories flooded back from our trip to New Orleans several years prior, where we were deeply moved by the destruction and pain caused by the hurricane. Reflecting on that journey, I began to connect it with the hurricane of challenges that ignited my entrepreneurial spirit. What brought a smile to my face in that moment was recalling the prayers we uttered to New Orleans and back, praying about the very endeavor we were now about to embark upon.

As we journeyed to meet the new team, our prayers were anything but random; they were specific and focused on the meeting and our desired outcomes. Before each prayer, we expressed gratitude to God for the chance to make a difference. Meeting the rest of the team allowed us to gauge who had connections with the supervisors, guiding our decisions on which groups of guys would work together.

Grass Clips

When you recognize the source of blessings,
you know precisely to whom gratitude is owed!

This contract differed significantly from our previous one, requiring a minimum of twelve tractors and separate trimming and litter crews. Each crew had to start at different points simultaneously. Additionally, we transitioned from mowing the highway three times a year to four times, reducing our completion time from around eighty days to under sixty days per cycle.

The Fruits of Expansion

"I can't believe you guys completed this work on time," the inspector remarked, noting that it had never been done punctually in the history of the contract. Everything seemed to align perfectly. It was as if we had finally turned the proverbial corner. It was the kind of moment that made everyone who ever dared to dream want to raise both fists and yell, "YES, YES, we did it!" With the first year of the contract completed and the equipment running smoothly, I felt a sense of relief. While we still had to follow up on payment statuses and occasionally drive to pick up payments promptly, we weren't in panic mode anymore.

Managing a large contract with a sizable team demands careful cash flow management. When payroll demands are substantial, borrowing isn't an option, especially without anyone to rely on for assistance. I rode every inch of those highways almost daily, ensuring we performed our job correctly. I pitched in to change out blades, deliver essential lubricants, offer encouragement, and frequently delivered bi-weekly payroll so crews wouldn't need to return to headquarters at the end of the week. My truck transformed into a quasi-mechanics truck, stocked with all the necessary tools to handle any field situation that arose.

Grass Clips

Amidst the comfortability of success,
it's crucial not to let the silence drown out your
plans for growth and retention.

As I often do, I began writing out new goals and aspirations, unwilling to settle for the current success. It's easy to become complacent with achievements, but I refused to fall into that trap. One day, as I looked in the mirror, a voice asked me a question that struck a chord. He said, "How many individuals are praying for an opportunity that you could offer if you weren't content with merely being 'okay'? That was my moment of realization. I felt the weight of the question and retreated to my desk to reflect. Expansion echoed in my mind, so I wrote down BML Inc. of North Carolina, South Carolina, and Tennessee.

I had the idea that we could replicate our operation in Georgia and expand into multiple states with a strategic plan. The next question was where to begin. I considered the areas where I had the strongest relationships and support. Perhaps, North Carolina or South Carolina, my home state. But where to start and which aspect of the industry to focus on? I began researching and came across the government website for procurement. I noticed they regularly issued solicitations for highway mowing. That's it... we'll start there and see how it goes.

Grass Clips

Making decisions never guarantees knowing the outcome, but the uncertainty shouldn't prevent you from making tough choices.

An Unexpected Loss

Shortly after we began the new highway contract, I received a call from one of the original partners from our first business, Double "L" Lawn Care. Sensing the seriousness in his voice, he asked if I was seated before delivering the news. I braced myself, knowing it wouldn't be good. He then told me the heartbreaking news: my Room Dog had cancer and wasn't expected to live much longer. In that moment, I felt a wave of emotions hit me like a ton of bricks. My heart shattered as I wept uncontrollably. I asked for some time to process the news before calling him back. The thought of losing someone I shared so many memories and dreams with was unbearable.

Before his passing, I made the journey to South Carolina every weekend, spending precious moments with him to lift his spirits. Then came the devastating call announcing his passing, leaving behind two young children. In an instant, the individual with whom I shared countless experiences, building our confidence and venturing into the lawn care business, was gone. While I remain convinced that moving forward alone was the right decision, I can't help but ponder how things might have unfolded if we had continued our journey together. Our friendship and brotherhood were genuine, and I often find myself reminiscing about the cherished moments we shared as roommates, companions, church volunteers, and business partners. These memories serve as a guiding light, helping me navigate life's complexities with clarity and purpose.

Chapter Seven

GRASS STAINS

The Cost of Excellence

"Steve, we will not approve another mile on this highway if it is not done perfectly," the inspector from our first highway mowing job pulled me aside to emphasize. She recounted how her supervisor instructed her to pull weeds in areas of the guardrail that were not properly maintained and asked her how it felt. Unsurprisingly, she expressed her displeasure and vowed it would be the last time she did such a task if she remained an inspector. From that point on, she and the other inspector rode us hard every single day, ensuring the highways were kept impeccably.

To meet these high standards, I would often return to work after everyone else finished for the day, redoing areas that didn't meet the expected quality. It was a lengthy process, and I wasn't sure if we would ever satisfy them. To work in the dark, I taped flashlights around the weed trimmer and attached a light to my hat. Eventually, we received a letter of recommendation from one of those inspectors, which provided validation for the contract awarded in our name. The letter praised our hard work and perseverance on that first opportunity. I was surprised by the inspector's endorsement considering how tough they had been on us. It taught me that what may seem like unjust opposition was just a manifestation of my fear of failure. By making others look good, they, in turn, will make you look good as well.

The Heartbeat

As things progressed smoothly at home, my focus turned to our expansion into North Carolina, indicating our entry into a new market. Delving into the intricacies of business in this state compared to Georgia became my priority. I diligently monitored their online bidding portal and reached out to various contacts for insights. After persistent efforts, I finally secured assistance, albeit with initial incredulity at my request for bid information spanning the past five years. Several weeks later, a box arrived, containing a treasure trove of bid responses from the past. You might wonder why I needed such a vast amount of data, and I'm glad you asked.

I delved into studying the bids and their patterns, aiming to grasp the pricing structures in North Carolina. Armed with this knowledge, I tailored our bidding numbers to align with our principles and practices. Concurrently, I researched the equipment required and closely monitored the procurement website. Several months down the line, when all the highway mowing contracts became available for bidding, I made the strategic decision to submit bids for every county, maximizing our chances of securing a contract.

Grass Clips

Success in any endeavor requires
not just a strategy to achieve it, but
also a strategy to sustain it.

One month later, we were delighted to receive notification that we had won a couple of contracts. Although uncertain as to why one contract did not proceed despite our victory, the chance to expand beyond Georgia's borders thrilled us. We were operating efficiently in our new location, and everything seemed to be going exceptionally well.

One day, during a visit to North Carolina, I received a call that shook me to my core. Upon answering, I was greeted by loud sobs. Despite my repeated inquiries asking, "What's wrong, what's wrong?" there was no coherent response, only continued crying. Sensing something amiss, I immediately went into prayer mode, asking God to see us through whatever problem lay on the other end of the line.

I stood in the middle of a field in rural North Carolina, holding the phone and praying fervently. After several minutes of inconsolable sobbing, my wife uttered the devastating words, "The baby is dead, there is no heartbeat." At that moment, I felt utterly inadequate as a husband and comforter. I was at a loss for words, unsure of how to provide solace. All I could do was listen in silence, my sorrow weighing heavily on me, my sobs stifled to spare her from hearing my pain.

After what felt like an eternity, all I could manage to say was, "I will be there as soon as I can." Hanging up the phone, I found myself once again grappling with God, questioning why He would allow such a tragedy to occur. This wasn't the first time we experienced loss; we endured a miscarriage a few years prior. But this time was different—my wife/business partner was close to three months along. I screamed at God for what felt like hours, pouring out my anguish and frustration. Yet, amid my turmoil, I felt a sense of reassurance wash over me, a gentle reminder that He is always in control and that everything would eventually be okay.

I chose to place my trust in Him. Without hesitation, I checked out of my room, provided instructions to the crew in North Carolina, and made my way back to Atlanta to be with my wife. Comforting her was not easy, but together we navigated through our grief, supporting each other every step of the way. When the time felt right, we decided to continue dreaming and holding onto hope for the future.

Grass Clips

Family holds immense significance in life, and
achieving balance in marriage is essential.
It is this equilibrium that decides whether
you'll thrive and conquer challenges
or falter and dwell in regret.

The Cost of Over-Night Expansion

We secured our first contract in North Carolina, which required us to procure new tractors equipped with flail mowers, a departure from our usual bush hogs. Flail mowers were designed to prevent rocks and debris from being ejected and featured multiple rows of teeth that finely cut the grass. Additionally, we needed side arm flails mounted with large hydraulic tanks to safely trim grass along highway ditch lines.

To continue, we encountered an unexpected setback when the foam-filled tires on our tractors began to damage the transmission and axles. Collaborating with the tractor dealership, we opted for super-thick tires called airplane retreads, which were touted to be virtually indestructible. To our surprise, on our very first day of operation, one of the operators inadvertently sliced a tire like a donut by placing the mounted tire jack incorrectly during a sharp turn. Despite being in Atlanta at the time, I had to quickly locate a dealer with the specialty tires and transport one to Fayetteville, NC, on the back of my truck.

Grass Clips

Organizational ineptitude comes with
a steep price and wastes time.

As I navigated the modest success we had achieved so far, I felt confident that nothing could derail us, but a storm of unprecedented magnitude was brewing. It wouldn't just affect me—it would engulf the entire United States. Like a tsunami, the financial markets crashed, and the housing bubble burst, leading to a widespread fallout affecting countless individuals, businesses, and financial institutions. While many suffered from what came to be known as the Housing Mortgage Crisis, it initially appeared that we might escape major hardship.

Despite encountering a few challenges, we believed we could manage them effectively. In fact, we were poised to continue growing, evidenced by a call offering us another contract in North Carolina. Overjoyed, I eagerly accepted without considering our financial standing or our current management capabilities, or lack thereof. Initially, our venture into North Carolina had been relatively smooth sailing, with everything seemingly falling effortlessly into place.

Push Back the Carrot

With four new tractors and experienced drivers familiar with the area's terrain, our team seemed well-prepared. Relocating our supervisor brought added benefits as they could easily visit metro Atlanta. Initially, cash flow issues were manageable, but gradually, challenges started to encroach upon our operation.

In our pursuit to expand, we purchased additional tractors outfitted with flail mowers. Regrettably, we deviated from our practice of buying new equipment, opting for four used units instead. This decision proved to be a disappointment, reminiscent of viewing real estate photos that make properties appear larger than they are. It underscored the importance of planning and making informed decisions rather than acting impulsively.

Under pressure to complete the work in the new area on time, we made some unwise decisions. The four used units we purchased turned out to be ineffective for our needs and essentially useless. On top of that, a couple of tractors vanished—they were stolen. To compound our challenges, our new supervisor had a serious accident, leaving us scrambling to find a suitable replacement. Additionally, connecting the cutter to the tractors requires high-pressure hydraulic lines, which often leak from the connectors.

It didn't take long for us to face a problem with the hydraulic line when it developed a small pin leak, which caused hydraulic oil to spurt out. To the untrained eye, it might have seemed like a minor issue, perhaps fixable with duct tape or by covering it with a thumb or hand. Unfortunately, the supervisor, unaware of the potential consequences, attempted to stop the leak using his hand. Almost immediately, he realized his mistake as the hydraulic oil pierced his skin, causing his hand to swell up like a balloon. He had to be rushed to the emergency room, where he narrowly avoided losing his hand due to poisoning. After this incident, he never returned to work, and from there, things began to unravel. The financial challenges we were already facing were compounded by rising gas prices, government cutbacks, increased home foreclosures, and a rising cost of living.

The final blow hit me like a sledgehammer when I received a chilling call informing me of a horrific accident involving one of our top tractor operators. A tractor-trailer had careened off the road, slamming into the back of the mower and trapping the driver between the seat and the steering wheel. In a panic, I immediately turned to prayer, pleading with God to shield him from harm and ensure he received the best possible medical care. They swiftly airlifted him to the nearest hospital for urgent treatment, while I reached out to my brother, who lived nearby, to provide support in the coming days. It was a harrowing ordeal, witnessing the pain and suffering of someone you care about deeply, yet feeling utterly helpless to alleviate their anguish.

Grass Clips

In the pursuit of goals, it's essential to recognize when to break free from the allure of dangling carrots and instead rely on strength and strategic resolve to chart a new course.

Despite the arduous journey, the gentleman eventually recovered, though not sufficiently to resume his previous work. By that time, our operations had long ceased. As I drove to North Carolina to salvage and take inventory of our equipment, I couldn't help but reflect on our journey. It's easy to feel engulfed by darkness when faced with challenges, but without light, we wouldn't even perceive the darkness. The contrast between success and failure becomes apparent only in the presence of light. Focusing solely on the dark clouds of adversity guarantees failure. Instead, we must keep our eyes fixed on the light of hope and resilience, steering our path towards success.

As challenging as it was, I knew that ending this chapter

of our journey was the right decision. It was time to cut our losses and focus on the financial storm brewing back home amidst the country's crisis. With the help of my best friend, we gathered our remaining equipment from various locations and transported them to a trusted ally's business premises.

I'm immensely grateful for the divine connections that have appeared in my life at precisely the right moments of need. My brother played a crucial role, meeting me at various locations to assist in gathering our equipment for transportation back to Georgia. Despite the challenges, facing voluntary repossessions for the third time brought about feelings of disgust and despair that never seemed to diminish. With around thirty tractors in our possession, I oscillated between feeling like we were on the ascent or plummeting back down to earth. Yet, I realized something greater.

Grass Clips

Failure isn't just a state of being it's also
where you allow yourself to believe you belong.
Our minds are delicate, capable of either trapping us
in poverty or propelling us toward success.
In such moments, belief becomes paramount.
Repeat after me: "I am a winner, and setbacks are
temporary because I refuse to give up!"

After concluding affairs in North Carolina, I delved back into ensuring our local Georgia operations ran smoothly without any hiccups. Despite the chaos we faced out of town, everything on the home front appeared to be progressing smoothly—until it wasn't. The storm we anticipated turned out to be even more severe than expected. We received notice that instead of mowing the highway four times a year, we would only be doing it once.

In addition, things became difficult with cash flow and the work scope. Now credit must be given where is due; we did receive notice asking if we would continue the work at the same rate, and we agreed to it. Though, when we began the work for the year, we realized it was no longer just grass we were cutting —it was small trees. This change caused us to hemorrhage cash flow daily as every aspect of the job took more than three times as long to complete. Despite this, we were still being paid the exact same rate as before the change. Frankly, I was fearful of letting go of the contract, especially considering we had held it for only three years at that point.

Staying hopeful amidst the economic downturn, we persevered until the end of the season, anticipating that the economy would turn around swiftly and fully fund the contract the next season. To navigate the financial challenges, my trusted business partner and wife devised a strategic plan for us to start paying off all our debts. Despite the loss of income from the highway contract, we remained committed to this plan. Additionally, we had secured several lucrative contracts with local school entities, which helped keep us afloat during this challenging period.

Flashback: A Marketing Genuis

Seated at our kitchen table, I called out to my business partner, who responded with a curious "Yes, Honey?" It was a familiar scene from our early days, where I'd often present my latest brainchild, already set on moving forward regardless. Knowing we lacked the budget for extensive marketing that could significantly alter our financial and business landscape, I pondered alternative strategies.

A thought occurred to me: if we couldn't afford to purchase mailing addresses, why not take matters into our own hands? We could simply hop into the car, strap our young son into his car seat, and drive through desirable neighborhoods. Armed with a pen and paper, we could jot down the addresses for a future mailer. It seemed like a feasible plan, and within a few weeks, we had gathered hundreds, if not thousands, of addresses. But just as we were about to execute the plan, another idea struck me: *Why spend money on stamps at all when we could simply leave flyers at each address?*

Eureka! It felt like a stroke of genius to me. Now, the question was what kind of flyers to use. Wanting to stand out, I proposed printing 3x5 cards featuring our logo and an invitation for a lawn care quote. I chuckled to myself, feeling like a marketing mastermind. But then, how would we distribute them? Suddenly, an idea popped into my head. What if we placed a few rocks in small Ziplock bags along with the cards and simply tossed them onto everyone's driveway? It seemed unconventional, but sometimes, the most effective ideas are the ones that break the mold.

When homeowners returned, they'd naturally find our surprise in their driveway alongside their mail. Opening the gift, they'd discover our service invitation, sparking an immediate interest. As we assembled thousands of packets at our advertising party, our hands worked tirelessly. With the help of my friend Rich Man, we set out to distribute them, tossing them onto driveways across neighborhoods. Our momentum hit a roadblock when a fearful homeowner mistook our harmless packets for something more sinister. In the climate of an anthrax scare across the US, they accused us of distributing toxic substances.

Grass Clips

Even when things seem foolproof at first glance, relying on quick fixes often leads to failure because they're typically not considered or planned out thoroughly.

Shaking my head in disbelief, I wondered why I hadn't anticipated such a possibility. After that call, we decided to halt our distribution of those packets altogether. The boxes filled with rocks and advertisements remained untouched in our office loft for many years to come. Little did I know that the following summer, just as we were emerging from one storm, our greatest challenge would emerge. Everything that unfolded thereafter would surpass any expectations I could have had. It became evident that God, as I have come to know and love, would undoubtedly have His hands on this situation.

Grass Clips

Being prepared for the unexpected is crucial.
Our ability to respond to adversity is sharpened
when we prioritize integrity and uphold it.
When you remain true to yourself consistently,
you don't have to pretend to be someone
you're not when faced with challenges.

After getting all the crews out of the shop and reviewing my various checklists for the day, I had a routine of heading to Smoothie King for my daily breakfast. Their slogan, "Chewing is Overrated," resonated with me, and I embraced the idea wholeheartedly. Not only did I feel healthier, but I also found that I had better focus. This morning ritual provided me with a moment to release the day's worries and clear my mind.

Arriving at Smoothie King, I placed my order, typically opting for one or two different smoothies, and waited on the side until my name was called for pick-up. As I grabbed my order from the attendant, my phone rang. Checking the caller ID, I noticed it was one of our supervisors. If I happened to be busy with something else, I typically let such calls go to voicemail, planning to return them once I had completed my current task.

This time, as I raised the phone to my ear and answered, I was met with sheer panic and fear on the other end. The supervisor's voice trembled as they repeated, "I think he's dead, Mr. Bromell, I think he's dead. My team member is dead!" In an instant, my smoothie slipped from my grasp and splattered on the floor, forgotten, as I rushed for the door. Jumping into my truck, I sped onto the interstate as if fleeing from a crime scene.

As the drink slipped from my hand, I felt a dense fog descend upon me, clouding my senses with uncertainty and dread. Piecing together the fragmented information, I gathered that one of our team members had been struck by a truck while working on the highway. Whether he had been severely injured or worse, dead, remained unclear. Turning to my usual response in times of crisis, I fervently prayed for God's protection over our team members and the crews on site, hoping for a favorable outcome.

If there was ever a moment to warrant a super speeder ticket, it was now. I couldn't even gauge how fast I was driving, desperate to reach the scene located near downtown Atlanta, normally thirty to forty minutes away. The disturbing news I received over the phone spurred me into action, and before I knew it, I was at the barricaded highway intersection. Holding up my drivers license, I identified myself as the owner of the company involved in the accident, and they waved me through.

Chapter Eight

BLOOD DRIVE

A Tragic Loss, Blood on My Hands

My jaw clenched and my stomach tightened with anticipation as I neared the accident scene. Scanning the area hastily, I spotted a group of our team huddled on the ground, while others gathered in solemn discussions. Firetrucks and ambulances dotted the scene. Immediately, I made my way to our guys, hearing whimpers and cries as I approached, a sound that pierced my heart and confirmed my fears: it was not good.

I was intercepted by our supervisor, and we immediately embraced, exchanging words of reassurance. As I stood before the guys, I went into prayer mode, seeking solace and strength from God. After finishing my prayer, I approached each of them, asking if they were alright. I received shaken nods in response. Despite their distress, I made sure to steer clear of the news crews present, focusing solely on comforting our team.

Somehow, I found myself shaking hands with people, feeling a sense of responsibility amid chaos.

Grass Clips

When you carry a greater power and presence, your aura speaks volumes, even in the darkest moments.

The medical examiner motioned me over to a covered bloody body, and I braced myself for the grim task ahead. Confirming my identity, he asked if I would identify the body. He explained the extent of the injuries, detailing how every bone had been shattered by the sheer force of the accident. The impact flung his body several hundred feet, illustrating the severity of the trauma. He was struck from behind while holding a weed trimmer, adding another layer of tragedy to the scene.

The force of the impact shattered the trimmer in half upon impact. As the medical examiner unveiled the body, I briefly glimpsed at our fallen team member's bruised and battered form. With a heavy heart, I nodded in acknowledgment that he was indeed part of our team. After that moment, everything became a blur. I can't recall anything, not even the lonely drive back to the office, which surely ranks among the loneliest drives of my life.

Struggling to find the words, I couldn't bring myself to call my business partner and wife to inform her of the tragedy, though I knew it was necessary. Upon returning to the office, I immediately made several phone calls to notify the family of our deceased team member urging them to speak with me as soon as possible. While gathering information, I learned that it was only his third day working with us. His bicycle, propped up against the wall in our bay, served as a poignant reminder of his presence.

Discovering that he had a wife and a young daughter under the age of three, I arranged for someone to call her again and request her presence at our office. I specifically asked them not to disclose thedetails of the situation, as I intended to speak with her upon her arrival. Conversing with his wife proved to be one of the most challenging tasks I've faced in both business and life, especially compounded by the language barrier between us.

Grass Clips

Great leaders should also be fluent
in universal emotional languages such as
sadness, regret, empathy, compassion,
understanding, and care.

As I entered the conference room, I could sense her apprehension, unsure of why she had been called in. The tension was palpable as I began to speak. With a heavy heart, I delivered the devastating news: her husband had been involved in a tragic accident and had not survived. The weight of her grief, filled the room, echoing in sobs that seemed to pierce the silence. On my watch, a man, a father, a husband, a good soul, had lost his life. Of all the things I wished I could undo in business; this was by far the most profound. In the days, months, and years that followed, I found myself navigating through the darkest period of my business journey.

Flashback: The New Narrative

"Mr. Steve, we need to speak with you." Those were the first words I heard as I answered the door to my hotel room. A couple of our guys wanted to share a huge concern they had while working on the highway that sounded almost unbelievable. "We were shot at on the exit ramp for the second time," they exclaimed, their words hitting me like a ton of bricks. "What did you say?" I needed a moment to process the gravity of their words. It seemed that while our team was diligently trimming on the highway, someone had been trying to instill fear and intimidate them.

Without a clear solution in mind, I assured them I would act and get back to them promptly. Our supervisor contacted local authorities, who then dispatched squad cars to monitor our crews for several days. The guys reported seeing an unmarked van lurking in the vicinity of their work areas, but once the police presence became apparent, the van disappeared. As I reflected on our circumstances, I couldn't shake the feeling of being plagued by close calls, challenging situations, and a seemingly relentless streak of misfortune.

In the aftermath of our worker's tragic death, the story made headlines on every local news station. In an era where local news could quickly go national via the internet, our ordeal garnered widespread attention. I grappled with intense emotions, and experienced waves of grief, regret, and self-condemnation as the leader of our organization.

Grass Clips

Leaders cannot shirk their responsibilities when faced with adversity, even if they wish they could evade the challenges like birds migrating with the changing seasons.

Things took a turn for the worse before any signs of improvement emerged. In the aftermath of the tragic accident, we granted all our crews a few days off to provide them with a chance to regain their composure and for us to process the unfolding events. To our dismay, the media attention persisted, with news crews appearing at our headquarters seeking interviews, particularly after it was revealed that the deceased worker was in the country illegally—an aspect that came as news to us, given our budding hiring process at the time.

Despite outsourcing the hiring process, the ultimate responsibility fell on my shoulders, and I couldn't deflect blame elsewhere. News crews clamored at our overhead door, seeking interviews, but I refrained from engaging, knowing it would likely lead to further complications. While it initially seemed that the situation would calm down after a few days, the country's heightened political climate regarding illegal immigration ensured that the issue remained in the spotlight. I found myself fielding calls from long-lost acquaintances, their concern indicating that the situation was far from resolved.

Despite segments of our workforce being of Hispanic descent and legally residing in America, perception trumped reality. Upon resuming work on the highway, our crews faced constant harassment from individuals demanding proof of their legal status. This hostile environment left them feeling unsafe and vulnerable to potential harm. Consequently, we lost most of our workforce in a short period, even though media attention on the incident dwindled, with only one news network continuing to cover the story.

One of the most troubling aspects of this entire incident was the lack of concern for the loss of life and the profound impact on the deceased worker's family. Instead, the focus was solely on his immigration status. Despite our lawyer issuing a sincere statement on our behalf, it seemed to exacerbate the situation rather than alleviate it. In one instance, a reporter relentlessly pursued one of our quality control managers that just happened to be the $39.99 Lawn Care Guy, thrusting a microphone in his face multiple times across various locations to elicit a sound bite.

They were convinced they had found a face to accompany the story, and they fully exploited it. Each report, including special investigative segments spanning multiple days, prominently featured his face and the pursuit. The sensational coverage persisted for weeks, even earning a prime spotlight one evening. My business partner and wife watched in horror as the focus shifted from a tragic accident to the looming threat of criminal charges due to our worker's immigration status.

We found ourselves with a fractured staff and an overwhelming amount of work to be done, prompting us to pivot our approach. With the help of new contacts, we arranged for several temporary staffing agencies to provide workers until we could establish a more permanent team. I must admit, it was a complete disaster. The labor required on the highway is grueling and demanding, often taking even the most eager workers at least two weeks to acclimate to the heat and physical exertion. Meanwhile, the news story continued to linger. Reporters were shadowing decision-makers from the department with whom we had contracted. I knew this would not bode well for us.

On a typical Sunday, I preferred to spend time with my family and attend church, avoiding work whenever possible. Given the uncertainties we were facing, I found myself in the office, sorting through paperwork and mentally preparing for the week ahead. While checking my email, I stumbled upon a message with the ominous subject line "thirty-day notice." With a sinking feeling in my stomach, I opened it, only to be shocked by the contents: we had been given thirty days to terminate our contract and halt all operations on the highway, including the removal of all equipment.

Grass Clips

*The true measure of a man lies not in his fear,
but in his faith when confronted by fear. Failure is not
defined by acknowledging what went wrong, but
by succumbing to the fear that lies within it.*

The notice continued, stating that any incomplete work would not be compensated. I exhaled deeply, then again, and silently repeated to myself, "Okay, God. Okay, God. Okay, God." I remained seated for what felt like an eternity, surrounded only by my thoughts in profound silence.

As the doorbell rang, I contemplated my usual strategy of ignoring it, enveloped in the darkness of my office. This time, fatigue and a sense of inevitability prompted me to confront whatever awaited. Until then, I avoided directly addressing inquiries about the accident and our involvement. On the news, other voices and faces represented us, prompting me to wonder about the consequences of my silence. Stepping into the foyer, I was met by two men with imposing firearms strapped to their hips, resembling large pistols.

By then, any lingering fear had dissipated, and I boldly opened the door to greet them. They inquired about my full name and requested to speak with me, to which I confirmed my identity. Inviting them inside, we exchanged pleasantries before they began their line of questioning. For a moment, I pondered whether to involve our lawyer, but ultimately decided to proceed with honesty, trusting that it would suffice.

They posed numerous inquiries, and I responded to each one with conviction, assuring them that we committed no wrongdoing, and that the accident was an unfortunate tragedy with widespread repercussions. Their primary focus was on whether we had thoroughly vetted the employee before hiring him and if we had utilized a national database for citizenship verification. While we had conducted vetting procedures, we had overlooked the implementation of the latest system available at the time, which ultimately proved to be our oversight in the entire ordeal. After a lengthy conversation, they appeared content with my responses, and they departed. I never encountered them again, which brought me a sense of relief. In the ensuing months, we faced lawsuits from numerous individuals and entities.

Grass Clips

Letting go of something you've invested in and cherished can be incredibly challenging, but sometimes it's necessary for your well-being. Seeking guidance from God can provide the clarity needed to release what no longer serves you. Trusting in a greater plan leads to unexpected blessings and opportunities.

Closing the email that Sunday in the fall of 2010, and delivering the devastating news of the contract's end to my wife and business partner weighed heavily on me. Yet, strangely, amidst the turmoil, there was a sense of relief. It offered a moment to breathe, to clear my mind, and to contemplate our next moves amidst the storm we were weathering.

With the contract back on the bidding market, numerous companies vied for the opportunity. Among them was the $39.99 Lawn Care Guy seemingly equipped to clinch the deal. Despite my hopes of supporting him as part of the team, his association with us through the news stories proved detrimental. It was a bitter pill to swallow. Yet, we had a responsibility to fulfill the remaining duties of the contract, regardless of our uncertain future with it.

I dusted off my work boots and assembled a team of six to tackle the highway project with a newfound sense of urgency. Despite the challenges and uncertainties, I was determined to ensure that we fulfilled our obligations with excellence. Working tirelessly from dawn till dusk, we poured our efforts into the task at hand, knowing that our financial well-being hinged on completing the required miles. My presence in the field not only motivated the team but also ensured that every moment was utilized efficiently, leaving no room for wasted time.

Despite the challenges, we made significant progress during those thirty days, completing much of the work required for the year. It was a grueling task, as we had to navigate through small trees instead of tall grass, which significantly slowed our progress. Despite the challenges, we persevered and continued to put in the hours until the very end. Surprisingly, I harbored no resentment or bitterness about losing the contract. I understood the circumstances that led to our removal and accepted them without complaint. But I couldn't shake off the disappointment in myself for allowing the situation to unfold as it did. A simple oversight in our processes could have spared us from this ordeal. Moreover, the weight of the tragic loss of life weighed heavily on my conscience knowing that a family was grieving because of it.

It was a tough moment, reminiscent of a similar situation in the past. I found myself once again drafting a letter to inform all our employees about the impending end of the contract and the cessation of work in just two weeks. Surprisingly, everyone seemed to take the news in stride, likely because they had been aware of the rumors and news reports circulating about our situation. My thoughts were scattered. All I yearned for was a sanctuary where I could find solace and tranquility. Unfortunately, such a place eluded me at that moment leaving me to navigate through this challenging period by relying solely on my faith to guide me forward.

Grass Clips

Amidst the chaos and adversity, it's crucial to train your mind and eyes to see beyond the apparent negativity. Even when everything seems to be moving in the opposite direction.

A New Name

"How about launching a new company with you as its President?" I proposed to my trusted business partner and wife. Intrigued, she encouraged me to elaborate. I highlighted the potential benefits—a clean slate, free from the burdens of debt and previous repossessions that were draining the life out of our ventures. The idea gained momentum as we envisioned the possibilities. After exploring numerous name options, we settled on a winner: Pro Cutters Lawnscapes, Inc. This fresh start seemed like the key to reclaiming our entrepreneurial vigor.

Choosing a name that clearly defined our identity yet could be scalable without relying on our last name, turned out to be a brilliant move. It marked one of our most strategic decisions. Once we secured the business license and completed the incorporation process, the focus shifted to creating a compelling logo and securing contracts. The realization hit hard—giving up meant forever remaining in the dark about what lay ahead. Conversely, pushing through revealed the next chapter.

After reviewing several logo designs, we settled on a sleek and simple cursive lettering logo. In a moment of inspiration akin to those "I stayed at a Holiday Inn last night" moments, I coined a catchy catchphrase: "All you need is grass... We'll take care of the rest!" Eager to secure business, we submitted a bid for a municipality project. They sought more extensive maintenance for their portion of the highway than the state transportation department allocated. Their focus was on ensuring the main roads within their city limits consistently looked well-maintained and presentable.

Undeterred by uncertainty regarding a new company's eligibility for bidding, we pressed forward, completing the necessary paperwork and submitting our bid. Several weeks later, a phone call came, and to our delight, they wanted to speak with us. Just like that, we secured our second major contract for the new venture. The first had been a contract to service nearly all the schools in one of the largest school districts in metro Atlanta following another contractor's default on their obligations. Our rapid growth saw us even subcontracting work from the established company BML Inc. Yet, progress hit a snag. Some unforeseen challenges emerged, and things didn't unfold as expected.

Despite a twinge of disappointment, a phone call brought a fresh sense of hope making me believe that some of the groundwork we laid for our company could still be salvaged. The new contractor reached out, seeking our assistance with the contract, and without hesitation, I affirmed our commitment. Just like that, we found ourselves partially back in the game, relieved of the stress that comes with being in charge and having direct scrutiny. While I've never shied away from the responsibilities of leadership, taking a step back at that moment felt truly rejuvenating!

Curious about why the owner had reached out, I inquired, and he simply stated that we were recommended based on the excellent work we previously delivered. The advantage of having our new company already operational became apparent as it served as the platform to restart operations seamlessly. We were assigned specific areas for maintenance, and the transition was smooth without any issues. We couldn't use all the staff we had previously employed due to the reduced workload; however, this turned out to be a blessing. It allowed us to reassemble the most dedicated team. Opting to work alongside the crews on occasions, I ensured that the work progressed seamlessly and met the satisfaction of inspectors.

Pro Cutters concluded the year as a subcontractor for the new company, and as far as I could tell, everything went smoothly. All tasks were completed on time, and we avoided any infractions in the work we carried out. To secure our place for the upcoming cutting season, I contacted the owner. Although his response seemed a bit unusual, he assured me he would provide details on the logistics later. I decided to patiently await further communication from him.

During the transition to a new home, I was also engaged in establishing the new company while responsibly winding down the operations of the previous one, maintaining the same level of integrity we had instilled in it. This proved to be an emotionally challenging period for me. I poured my heart and soul into crafting a brand synonymous with excellence, and it was disheartening to witness its gradual closure.

While gazing over our deck one day, I received a phone call from the company owner we had been subcontracting with, delivering the news that they no longer required our assistance moving forward. Despite expressing gratitude for our help, he explained his decision to handle all the work with his in-house crew now that he was familiar with the area. The impact of his words felt like a gut punch as if my insides might spill out onto the very deck I stood upon. I moved the phone, staring at it momentarily, hoping it was just a dream.

Unfortunately, it was not a joke; it seemed to be over just like that! I wandered around in a daze. The sense of bewilderment lingered for what felt like an eternity. I kept questioning myself about what had transpired. While expressing gratitude to him and assuring our availability if needed, I felt a surge of internal steam, as if frustration was emanating from every pore of my body. Strangely, my anger was not directed at him but at myself. In my mind, I hadn't been diligent in tending to what I was entrusted to shepherd. The weight of being perceived as a diminished provider and an outright failure weighed heavily on me, and my mind raced to figure out how we could recover from this setback.

My mind harkened back to the past when out of the blue I asked my wife how she wanted to live. A curious question you may ask, however it would prove necessary for me to know just how hard I would need to work and the sacrifices that would need to be made for that lifestyle. I then asked her to create a spreadsheet showing what our company would look like making one million dollars per year. That number remains in my memory, $83,333.33 per month. At that very moment it seemed light years away!

With the phone clutched in my hand, the daunting reality of paying bills and sustaining a business after losing a significant portion of our income in the blink of an eye weighed heavily in my mind. Taking a deep breath, I straightened up and uttered, "God, I trust You. What doesn't kill me must make me stronger. With God, all things are possible. If God is for you, then who can be against you?" I repeated these phrases until doubt dissipated from my mind.

After gathering my thoughts, I summoned the courage to share the news with my wife. True to form, she met the situation with resilience, expressing some of the most vital words a wife can offer her husband: "Honey, I believe in you, and I know we will be fine." Those words were precisely what I needed to hear.

Grass Clips

*One of the paramount keys to success in marriage
is the buy-in and unwavering support from your spouse.
This should never be taken for granted as this connection
and shared belief can transform failure into a mere
comma, signaling a continuation of hope!*

Fortunately, we had other sources of business-related income to fall back on, but they paled in comparison to what we had lost. The situation was further compounded by the unexpected loss of another subcontracting job. In my quest for answers and growing impatient as I waited, I took matters into my own hands *(a tendency I admittedly have)*. I began scouring online platforms for job opportunities that would allow me to work as an independent contractor or employee utilizing some of the trucks we owned for transporting goods.

Landing an interview swiftly, I put on one of my suits, firmly believing in the adage "dress to impress." As I sat in the interview, responding to every question posed to me, memories of the early years in business resurfaced. I recalled attempting to return to Federal Express, only to be halted by an internal voice warning me that if I went back, I would never leave.

I poured my heart into the interview, and the company owner was genuinely impressed. Unfortunately, he was perhaps too impressed, realizing that my level of experience far exceeded the requirements for the position. While I felt a tinge of disappointment, it served as reassurance that God hadn't called me backward but had orchestrated a brief pit stop to recalibrate my A-game.

It took several years for my wife and business partner to genuinely believe that I had taken such drastic steps. She couldn't fathom me stepping back or, under any circumstances, working a regular job. What she didn't fully grasp was the weight of failures pressing on me and the understanding that pride means nothing to a man who can't support his family.

Chapter Nine

SCALPED

Your Honor

As we stepped onto the elevator to attend one of the depositions related to the tragic accident, I took a deep breath and let out a sigh. I couldn't help but wonder when this nightmare would finally come to an end and what life might look like several years beyond that day. Entering the conference room, I observed a group of lawyers huddled around a substantial conference table. The thought crossed my mind that we might seem like fresh prey to what I assumed were legal vultures, but I recognized that they were merely carrying out their professional duties, and there wasn't a personal vendetta against us.

With several cases on our plate, this one stood out as the largest. I courteously pulled out my wife's chair, exchanged greetings with everyone around the table, and took my seat. As expected in depositions, we navigated through routine questions for many of which they likely already knew the answers.

A few inquiries I found to be rather intrusive. We continued answering truthfully. Unexpectedly, the tone shifted, and the questions turned confrontational, directed primarily at my business partner and wife, Shawn.

The questions took such a nasty turn that I could sense Shawn growing increasingly frustrated and upset. It reached a tipping point where I halted the meeting by pushing back my chair and rising to my feet. I'm certain I had that unmistakable look in my eyes that husbands get when defending the honor of their beloved against a disrespectful foe. Standing tall, I firmly conveyed that their line of questioning was inappropriate, particularly considering my wife's pregnancy, and I would not tolerate it any longer. I made it clear that if they wished to proceed, they needed to tone it down. No authority or individual has the right to speak to my wife in a demeaning manner, and I would not allow it under any circumstances.

Following the deposition, the case was settled, and Shawn skillfully negotiated terms to ensure they couldn't pursue us personally or harm our business in the future. It felt like, at last, the legal turmoil might be concluding, albeit with the lingering burden of our financial downfall. The metaphorical house of cards had collapsed, creating a perfect storm. I found myself often on the deck, contemplating and seeking answers from God about what lay ahead. Burdened with substantial debt and limited prospects of resolving it in our current circumstances, we ultimately embraced the difficult decision to let go of everything.

Holding onto depreciating assets that act as burdens around our necks is counterproductive to the journey of rebounding success. Recognizing this, I made the decision to release those former assets and dedicated myself to repaying every individual and business I had connected with, irrespective of the time it might take. Over several years, I fulfilled this commitment. Yet, it's essential to note that qualities like character and integrity are not something that should be turned on and off; they remain paramount regardless of the circumstances.

A former employee, whom I had mentored and happened to be the one who called me the day of the tragic accident, reached out to inform me about an opportunity. He expressed feeling overwhelmed by his workload, and after considering his predicament, I offered my expertise. We reached an agreement, and I started working for him representing his business and servicing his client. You might wonder why I chose to work for a former employee, but the truth is, I needed to remind myself that growth often occurs when you take a step back and are willing to humble yourself.

Grass Clips

Never think you are too good to help others.
The moment you start believing you are above such
acts is the moment you hinder your potential
for growth and progress.

Being an early riser often reminded me of an old Army TV commercial that aired across the US: "We do more before 9 a.m. than most people do all day." Taking this sentiment to heart,

I made it a habit to start my mornings super early, crafting schedules for our few maintenance crews working on various contracts. Despite my dedication to the job, I found myself still in a funk and unwilling to face any of our team members. Instead, I would leave the schedules in their trucks and hit the road for work on my own. In a somewhat twisted way, I felt this self-imposed isolation served as a form of penance for what I perceived as dropping the ball with the tragic accident even though I knew it wasn't my fault.

I couldn't shake the realization that the tragic events could have been prevented, and the responsibility squarely rested on my shoulders. Despite my intimate knowledge of all the interstate systems in metro Atlanta, I consciously avoided getting on any of them for over a year. The mere thought of navigating those highways served as a painful reminder of what we had lost, and the memories were too raw to confront. Finding solace, I turned to basic lawn maintenance as a form of therapy, fully immersing myself in the task. Armed with my trusty notepad, I jotted down the issues that caused our setback and strategized on how to eventually right the ship.

During my time on each property, I took moments to pray and meditate, expressing gratitude to God for His creation and the opportunities He provided for me. There was a profound joy in these moments, realizing how much I loved the simple act of cutting grass. Simultaneously, tears would stream down my face, not out of sadness, but from a deep sense of gratitude for all I had overcome. I understood that one day, this very moment would become a poignant teaching memory.

When my oldest son expressed his desire to visit for the

summer and his need for a vehicle, I proposed a win-win scenario. I offered to match whatever he earned working in the business and assist him in finding a vehicle. This arrangement not only provided him with an opportunity to contribute and earn but also allowed us to spend much needed father-son time together.

Encouraging our children through incentives nurtures character and imparts the lesson that significant achievements come with a price. To attain something worthwhile, one must demonstrate commitment through unwavering dedication and a strong work ethic. The results will follow.

During that summer, working alongside him taught me a valuable lesson: parents cannot impose their passions onto their children and expect them to abandon their pursuits. It's crucial to allow them the space to discover and follow their path.

He initially worked two to three days a week allowing time to acclimatize to the hot weather and strenuous work. Over the next couple of weeks, he gradually increased his workdays until we settled on a four to five-day workweek. Working with him was a fulfilling experience providing opportunities for long talks during our travels from site-to-site. The highlight of those times was our lunch conversations.

As the summer ended, we sat in a restaurant, and he began questioning the purpose behind our endeavors. I explained this journey was a form of self-imposed discipline, a way for me to redirect my focus and regain control of my thoughts after the challenges we previously faced. I assured him we weren't giving up by any means, but rather, I needed this break for preparation. Breaks don't have to be negative when there's purpose in your plan, and taking a pause doesn't imply irreparability. It's common to find ourselves spending excessive time second-guessing and contemplating giving up when life throws a challenge our way and convincing ourselves that we can't recover from the pain or disappointments. Yet breaks in bones typically make them stronger when healed.

Grass Clips

In life, invest more time and energy in
the stages of repair than you do in the stages
of disappointment and complaining.

"Steve, are you alright?" inquired the manager of a nearby repair shop as I was delivering a piece of equipment. I turned and looked directly into his eyes, responding, "Yes, everything is going fantastic." He mentioned that he hadn't seen me in full working uniform for quite a while and was just wondering if something happened. Aware that news of the tragic events had spread, I smiled and assured him that all was well. I added that when I was ready, we would embark on a solid trail of comeback.

Towards the end of the summer, as my son and I were having lunch, he asked me a simple but direction-changing question. "Dad, when are you going to move out of this so-called self-administered punishment phase of work?" I looked at him sternly but with a smile and replied, "Son, when I feel as though it is time. I will never go back to this point ever again in life."

Grass Clips

Conviction is a potent force, not just when you think it, but when you are bold enough to say it and stand on it.

At that moment, my path forward became clear, and I received a resounding answer from God that the time for a comeback was near. It was approaching, and I anticipated it would be an awe-inspiring spectacle to witness. My son, Michael Jr., received his vehicle and returned to school at Indiana University, while I continued to service the properties for my mentee for several more months.

A Comeback

While I felt my confidence growing in my current work, I sensed that my purpose had not yet been fully realized, prompting me to explore other opportunities. Returning to the well of giving, I sought to alter the tides in our favor. Upon learning about a business conference in Atlanta, sponsored by a group I vaguely knew about, I decided to purchase two tickets—one for myself and another to be given away, though I hadn't identified the recipient.

During a conversation with a fellow church member, someone I hadn't had the chance to know well, we exchanged information. Later that week, I reached out to him and extended an invitation to the conference with no strings attached. I made it clear that we didn't need to stick together during the event; I simply wanted to sow a seed into his life.

While we were talking, he mentioned he wanted to do business but was stuck due to the economic downturn a few years prior, a sentiment anyone who lived through 2008–2010 would understand. Arriving at the meeting alone, I could feel my heart racing in anticipation that someone would share a nugget so bright I could not miss the moment if I tried, or I would meet someone who could help propel me forward. I wish I could tell you that one of these scenarios unfolded, but it was not to be. Don't get me wrong; the meeting was fantastic, and the speakers were truly motivating. I did not leave empty-handed, and I surely got my fix, but not to the level I was anticipating.

Grass Clips

Stay open to God. You can't imagine how He works on your behalf and in what form His blessings will manifest.

During our lunch break at the conference center, with several restaurants to choose from, I decided to grab some food and invited my new friend from church to join me. Upon entering, I noticed a table with some familiar faces from our church, and they waved us over. We engaged in extensive business discussions, and I left that lunch feeling incredibly energized about my future. Before leaving, I collected all the tickets, and without anyone noticing, I covered the cost of everyone's lunch and walked away. Practicing generosity and sowing seeds often opens the door to receiving. At my core, I embody the qualities of a giver and a sower. At that moment, I believed positive developments were starting to unfold.

"Steve, your life will be ruined if you enter the military instead of attending college," my high school English/ Journalism teacher warned, it's a refrain that echoes in my mind during setbacks. Remembering her words, I still clung to hope, brushed off the negativity, and recalled the discipline instilled in me by the military. Each morning, I woke up without an alarm clock, armed with the will to conquer anything. I held firm that nothing could obstruct my purpose, reciting to myself the mantra: "Read, Believe, and Succeed." Sensing a shift, I knew something significant was brewing, destined to shape the remainder of my business journey.

I retrieved my trusty notepad and started jotting down the names of major corporations with which I aspired to collaborate. I would gaze at the list daily, uncertain of the how but steadfast in my belief that it would materialize. Switching the lights back on in the office, I re-engaged with the small team of employees we had at that time. As New Year's approached, I attended the New Year's Eve Service at church.

That night remains etched in my memory. While walking down the hallway, one of our Pastors stopped me and said, "Your business will quadruple this year." Then, she walked away. I held onto those words, pondering how she could grasp what was in my heart and the projects I was diligently pursuing. Not long after that encounter, I received an invitation to teach an entrepreneur class, but there was a catch. I had to co-teach it with two other people. Initially, I scoffed at the idea of having someone look over my shoulder.

Despite my initial hesitation, I accepted the challenge with gritted teeth and began teaching a class named "Dream Builders: The Business Life of Joseph." This experience led to two friendships that I will always cherish. These friends encouraged and prodded me to delve deep into the well of my experiences, knowing that it was meant for the sole purpose of sowing into other businesses. Drawing lessons from the life of Joseph, I provided demonstrations that affirmed my life statement: "I will give my way to success." As the class progressed, I was introduced to an executive from one of the corporations on my list.

The Pitch

Events continued to unfold in our favor. Soon, my business partner and I found ourselves in a high-rise elevator, impeccably dressed and with a surreal feeling enveloping the moment. Had I finally arrived? The straightforward answer is NO; nonetheless, presenting our company filled me with immense joy. Every journey starts with a step, and at this juncture, it felt like I had taken quite a few. Alongside my trusted business partner and wife, armed with our PowerPoint Presentation, we delved into our pitch. Exiting that expansive building, I was on cloud nine, and one might have mistaken our accomplishment for hitting the lottery.

"Do not bet against us!" I exclaimed in a lighthearted and jovial manner to a room brimming with executives as I pitched our business. This response followed their inquiry about where I envisioned our business in the next five to ten years. Unwaveringly, I stated, "Twenty million dollars stronger." The room experienced a brief pause, eyes widened, and they questioned, "Really?" I acknowledge that, for some, it might not appear substantial, and others may deem it an ambitious goal.

At the time, our business was generating a couple of hundred thousand dollars a year. To put things into context if someone told me I could make over six figures cutting grass when I first started, I would have been over the moon with that news. I never take for granted the amount one makes doing honest work for honest pay. Whether you break six figures, seven, eight, or nine, celebrate it and stay humble because greater growth may just be around the corner!

Grass Clips

There is never a penalty for dreaming big, but there is one for not dreaming at all!

On my way out, I grabbed some business cards and committed to staying in contact until something came up. Since I wasn't content with just waiting for opportunities to come to me, I decided to start making waves in other areas. Then, one day, my friend presented a situation to me. He needed a location to host a meeting of his. Being the giver that I am, I leaned over and responded, "Why don't you have your meeting at our office? We have two conference rooms, and it will be free for you." Afterward, I reconsidered my statement and suggested, "Better yet, schedule your meeting, and I'll stay around until you're done. Don't delay what is in your heart to do." He responded with "You are so right, and I will take you up on your offer."

On the day of his meeting, I was in my office with the lights on this time. I was working on some paperwork when he knocked on my door. I answered, and he asked me if I wanted to sit in on the meeting just to hear what he had going on. Initially, I shook my head, thinking I did not want to be inserted into something that was not meant for me. He left the invitation open and assured me it was okay to stop by if I wanted. Unsure why, I decided to go down the hallway, and to this day, I am so glad I did. The meeting turned out to be a roundtable discussion about real estate, some unique building ideas, and general business opportunities. The best part was being introduced to a couple of guys who would play a crucial role in our comeback. The overall meeting was highly informative, leading to future business in a completely different area than landscaping.

Grass Clips

You don't need to know everyone;
just treat those you do know well, and they will
introduce you to those you should know.

Let's Bid Again

In the landscaping industry, most contracts have expiration dates, and one never knows whether they will fulfill the entire contract or be the winning bid the next time it is out on the open market. Moreover, other entities routinely bid lower than the previous year. This can be a tricky endeavor due to factors like equipment inflation, maintenance costs, repairs, and labor expenses. As you can imagine, it is common for new firms to secure a contract and underestimate the exact requirements needed to complete the job.

This primarily occurs with larger contracts. Consider this: Which firms have the resources to staff contracts that require forty to two hundred people at one time? This demands careful planning, strategic thinking, and precise execution. With this scenario in mind, we decided as a company never to get upset if we lost a contract. Instead, our goal would always be to leave a property looking better than it did before we took over. After giving that some thought, I realized that no one owns contracts forever, and we should be grateful for the opportunity while it lasts. Also, if you keep a clean and jovial heart with loss, you never know when it may come back to you.

That last statement is exactly what happened with one of the major contracts we had. We were servicing about thirty properties. The contract ended, and we informed them, including the inspectors, just how much we appreciated the opportunity to serve them and their clients. Shortly after the partnership ended, we received a call to see if we could not only take back the ones we lost, but also an additional forty properties.

Grass Clips

*Doing things with an excellent attitude and
work ethic will propel you further.*

As I settled back into the office environment, most days I would scan bidding portals to see if any new opportunities were posted. I wanted to ensure that when one became available it would be the right fit for us, I would have enough time to research and put out the best response possible. Just like in a good "Rocky" movie, where you watch him get beat up badly, you most certainly know somehow, he will make a comeback. While there was no "Eye of the Tiger" song playing when I saw the caption of the bid on the screen, I almost fell out of my chair.

The contract we lost due to the tragic accident was unexpectedly back up for bid after only a year and a half. To say I was stunned would be a vast understatement. While the current company seemed to be doing an outstanding job, the contract owners intended to include additional work, necessitating the bid to be reopened. Moreover, the selection process would now involve a point system to determine the awardee. After gathering my bearings, I printed out the entire contract and meticulously read through every word, highlighting new language and nuances to ensure a comprehensive understanding of their requirements and our capability to fulfill them.

As I neared completion of the proposal, it struck me that the requirement specified a company with a minimum of three years' experience in business. At the time of the bidding, our new company would just be entering its third year, having allowed the previous one to slowly fade away. To dispel any uncertainty, I promptly called and followed up with an email. The response received the next day left me seated at my desk in sheer astonishment. If anyone saw me during that moment, I'm certain I appeared pallid. I lingered there for an extended period, gazing into space, processing the unexpected turn of events.

Chapter Ten

A JOURNEY OF NO'S

The Rewards of Integrity

One crucial lesson I've acquired over the years is that if something is destined for you, there are often multiple paths for it to unfold. Also, I firmly believe that loyalty, when handled appropriately and boundaries are respected, shouldn't have an expiration date. Refuse to let doubt dictate the beginning or end of your journey. Before delving into the next part, it's important to note that loyalty is a defining trait of my character, often to the extent of being considered a fault.

Upon entering a contract with another company to perform work under their banner, my policy is to abstain from bidding on that work in the future—unless, of course, they withdraw from the project. Despite previously securing the contract, I would have been willing, albeit with a touch of wounded pride, to collaborate with the company that ultimately won the project, as we had done for several months before we were unexpectedly let go. It's important to note that there was no lingering animosity between us, only a sense of disappointment on my part, which I had largely overcome.

The current contractor approached me to assess our interest in bidding, and I explained that we couldn't participate due to not meeting the stipulated requirements. I expressed willingness to collaborate if he had proposed a partnership, complete with written and signed agreements to avoid any abrupt changes. That proposition never materialized. Despite this, I maintained an open line, offering assistance if needed. At this point, I hadn't communicated with the $39.99 Lawn Care Guy for several months. A once robust mentorship and friendship now had me questioning whether it had run its course.

Grass Clips

Relationships are a blessing.
Good ones should be cherished and guarded
with passion, as they are scarce
throughout our lives.

I learned that he lost all his contracts due to the economy and hadn't managed to rebound. The disappointment of not securing the contract when we received the thirty-day notice left a bitter taste in his mouth, especially given his excellent past work for the entity. His company, which I considered one of the premier up-and-coming ones in the industry, seemed to have ended abruptly. Despite reaching out with words of encouragement, I couldn't connect with him directly, leaving messages in the hope of trying again.

Despite numerous messages, I stopped reaching out and began praying for him whenever he crossed my mind. Considering the potential opportunity, I decided to make one last attempt to discuss it with him. Miraculously, he answered on the first ring, akin to a fourth quarter Hail Mary! Our calls never started conventionally with a simple hello; instead, we exchanged affirmations like "Strong, Faithful, Wise, and Prosperous Man of God," sometimes lasting three to five minutes. Interestingly, these calls often turned into impromptu prayer services, momentarily sidelining the initial reason for the call.

Due to his nature, the calls typically involved him praying for me or whoever had reached out to him. This time, the student was encouraging the teacher. I urged him to break free from the funk he was in and give me his full attention, which he willingly did. Respect has a unique way of leveling the playing field, enabling boldness in your interactions with those in your tribe. I inquired if he was prepared to re-enter the game, shaking off the dust accumulated during almost two years of being knocked down.

Grass Clips

Having the privilege of a mentor is an opportunity to absorb every bit of information they share, as you never know when they might need you to reciprocate and pour into them.

Another Chance

I had no precise plan on how this would unfold, but I was committed to assisting him in any way possible, even if, in the end, he chose to venture solo. You might be curious about my motivation. When someone consistently advocates for you, there comes a time when you should be ready to reciprocate. Whenever I sought advice or needed words of encouragement, he consistently stood by me. Over the years, I observed and learned from the $39.99 Lawn Care Guy, serving as his mentee, and actively implementing changes to enhance our company.

I then contacted my mentee, and we joined forces to strategize our approach. As I faced myself in the mirror, a persistent question demanded an answer: "Are you willing to wholeheartedly support him, without complaint, even if you disagree with the decisions made?" Given my strong loyalty, my response was an unequivocal commitment to stand by him, offering my assistance without reservation. We worked diligently to compile a comprehensive packet, ensuring meticulous attention to detail. With several contracts available for bidding, we chose to submit proposals for three of them.

Everything went smoothly until the final day when we were assembling all the information into binders, carefully double-checking to ensure nothing was overlooked. As he had contributed to the work, he was familiar with the bid numbers, and my responsibility was to organize the comprehensive package. We utilized every available second to meet the deadline and were confident in our submission. I didn't accompany them to submit the bid, so I wasn't aware of the events during that time. Upon their return, he requested a few minutes with me and candidly conveyed that we would proceed only with my involvement, excluding my mentee.

I was thoroughly perplexed, and he insisted that I needed to trust him, assuring me it would be for the best. I felt a deep sense of regret because, at that stage in my business journey, I likely wouldn't have made the same decision he did. We invested significant time together strategizing and outlining various scenarios in case we secured one of the bids. This sudden shift caught me off guard. I had to revisit my commitment to do whatever was asked without questioning, realizing that I was being tested sooner than I had anticipated. Although my mentee was understandably disappointed, there was nothing we could do at that point, especially since we hadn't been awarded anything and the likelihood seemed like a long shot, to say the least.

About a month later, the results were in, and we won one of the bids! The contract was almost four times more than our original one, with additional work included. Just like that, we were not only back in business but with an opportunity to exceed previous levels. The $39.99 Lawn Care Guy was back, and the question lingered whether the offer for me to be his sidekick still stood. You might wonder why I framed it that way. Well, it's one thing to speculate, but when you have a contract in hand, dynamics tend to change. I had been around long enough to experience promises that evaporated, and unfortunately, I had done it once myself. The bottom line was that I was prepared for either outcome, and my heart was in the right place.

After his call and the deal was sealed, I meticulously crafted a list of everything required to meet the contract specifications.

While we had a preliminary list, we needed to fine-tune it and devise a strategy for efficient management. It wasn't just my tractors; all of ours had been repossessed, including his. Nearly all the trucks were gone too, except for a handful that I managed to retain. Though I had saved a bit, it was clear that what I had wouldn't come close to what was needed.

I proposed that we take a moment to assess precisely what we would need and the associated costs. We reached out to two other acquaintances, assigning them as frontline managers to assist in organizing crews and planning routes. Utilizing a van, we started breaking down the routes to determine the required number of crews to meet the contract deadlines upon commencement. Simultaneously, we arranged meetings with potential investors introduced by one of the managers.

This is a crucial point, so pay attention. As I mentioned earlier, my trusted business partner and I resolved not to finance our future under any circumstances. Now, with a contract in hand and the need for 25+ tractors, 20+ trucks, 150+ workers, and sufficient capital to sustain the project for a minimum of three months *(you get the picture)*, our stance was put to the test. Be cautious about the principles you choose to stand upon, as you might find yourself challenged sooner than you think. At that moment, you'll face a choice—whether breaking your word is justified by the potential results.

The total cost for all the required brand-new equipment exceeded two million dollars. It's crucial to understand that we lacked both the capital and the credit needed to secure financing. Fortunately, one of our designated front-line managers had an extraordinary ability to attract people and maintain valuable connections just a phone call or two away. I always admired his gift in this regard and felt fortunate to have him on our team.

Three Strikes

He made some calls, and with the assistance of a dynamic individual I have known for years, we secured four meetings with influential financial leaders. I meticulously crafted a business plan, outlining our numbers and requests, and offering a 30% return on any financial assistance within six months. While it might sound too good to be true, I genuinely believed we would be reviewing offers and selecting the one that best suited our needs. The punchline turned out to be on me. Today my trusted business partner and I chuckle about those meetings attended by the $39.99 Lawn Care Guy and me.

Later, we had a meeting with the bank owner who appeared quite interested until I made it clear that we neither qualified nor desired to finance any loans. With a raised brow, he pondered for a moment and responded, "Well, I might be willing to assist you guys, given the high recommendations and endorsements you've received, if you're willing to sign life insurance policies for yourselves and your spouses." My mind immediately conjured images of some godfather-style backroom deal, and with sincere thanks, we politely declined.

We continued our conversations, but in my mind, I marked this as strike one. In baseball, you get three strikes, and then you're out. However, in the first inning, you'll typically get at least two more at-bats with three *additional* strikes. The next two strikes came just as fast, and the pitcher didn't seem to have broken a sweat. We switched our stance, opting for a different method, hoping to break the giant down into bite-sized pieces, and anticipating better responses.

For the next bat, I went alone, armed with the business plan in my briefcase, dressed sharp enough to be in a casket *(I felt like getting in one after the meeting)*, and with the confidence of knowing the deal would be done at hello. I walked into the expansive Ford dealership showroom with the strut of an iconic wrestler. I then asked to see the manager. All eyes were on me, wondering who in the world this guy was. Once I sat down with my presentation, it all went downhill from there.

I now laugh uncontrollably at that day, but then, I felt like an earthworm with no purpose. It sounded like a chorus to me, with everyone seemingly laughing at what I was asking for. Requesting over fifteen trucks with no down payment and no financing, solely on the strength of my word to pay them back in six months, seemed like an audacious feat. You may be wondering if I was under the influence of drugs given the nature of my request, but I was not. I sincerely believe I adequately explained what we needed for our contract, and they understood as well. I would have never gone if I thought otherwise.

Crushed and humiliated, I brushed it off after a few hours and went back to the drawing board. Time was becoming a factor, and we needed to make something happen quickly, or we would be in jeopardy of throwing in the towel before we could even get it dirty. I had one more meeting lined up with a former NBA player known for philanthropy. Despite not being directly related to our industry, we both stood firm on the principle found in 2 Corinthians 9:10, "He gives seed to the sower."

I was scheduled to meet him at a game, and he agreed to extend five to ten minutes to hear me out. I presented our pitch, highlighting the 30% return in six months, and he graciously declined. I thanked him for his time and then tried to enjoy the game as best I could.

Before we embarked on the series of meetings, we ensured we looked the part, which meant investing in some up-to-date clothes. I sent my friend to a fashion expert I knew at the time to assist us. I've always believed that when you look good, you're likely to feel good and almost certainly feel better. Despite the string of rejections, I contemplated taking more of a back seat. Still, I was reminded that I had given my word to give all I had to make this work and get him back to a good place. We were exasperated and wondering how we would pull this rabbit out of our hat because that is what it would take as time was rapidly winding down.

Cold calling or even warm calling people always made me uncomfortable, evoking memories of childhood experiences on welfare, using food stamps, and feeling humiliated. Now I realize that some of my greatest breakthroughs in life came when I willed myself to do what was difficult. Fueled by the power of bold prayers, I decided to visit the place where we purchased our second wave of tractors, which were repossessed later unfortunately.

I had a relationship with the owners, and even though I typically worked with the sales manager assigned to our county, I knew I would need to speak to the owners directly. After some small talk, we got down to business, and the question was posed, "What can I help you with, Mr. Bromell?" With painful honesty, I laid out our needs and impending deadline. There were a few minutes of silence, and just briefly, all those other nos played before me. I closed my eyes, willing those negative thoughts away.

He finally spoke and said, "How about I think about this some more and get back to you shortly." I stood up, shook his hand, and expressed my appreciation for him taking time out of his schedule to meet with me. The waiting game can consume you if you are not careful, so I reported back to my new partner and said there was no need to sit on our hands. We had more things to get done. I started putting routes together. Then, we had an idea. We decided to let the two managers have their own teams. This would allow them to make way more money than working with a salary cap.

It was simple: they would be paid based on how much work they completed efficiently on their routes. We would also require them to have their own equipment, which would bring better accountability and, as a result, minimize part of the overall equipment we would need to obtain ourselves. As we thought about it, we created six routes with the same premise: everyone would run their own crew as part of the team. Based on everyone's capability and geographical location, we assigned each of them a route.

All Things Work Together

We were moving quickly, and things began to fall into place despite the elephant in the room: "What are we going to do about the additional 12 to 15 tractors we need?" That was answered, at least partly, with a call I received asking if I could come back to the heavy duty equipment dealer for a discussion. Upon arriving, the owner said he would help us, and I held my breath wondering just what that would mean. While I was smiling inside, he said, "I will give you the tractors, and you can pay us directly with no financing." Of course, it would cost us a little more, but I did not have an issue with that at all. He then mentioned the only condition would be that if the contract went south, we'd return the tractors with no strings attached. YES! YES! YES!, you heard it right—just like that, we were in pole position to succeed. In addition, they offered for us to buy back several of our previously repossessed tractors for pennies on the dollar! Following that pivotal moment, events rapidly gained momentum as we successfully negotiated with a local gas station our company had been collaborating with for several months. We reached an agreement for a gas supply, committing to payment every two weeks. The owner even expressed his appreciation for our continued support of his business.

The phones rang incessantly, and former employees of the previous contractor, who were knowledgeable about the new contract, reached out offering their valuable assistance. Finally, the $39.99 Lawn Care Guy signed the contract, propelling us into action. It's intriguing how, when circumstances take a turn for the worse, everything negative seems to gather, almost mocking our misfortune. On the flip side, I firmly believe that when things go right, positivity also congregates, leading to unexpected benefits that surpass imagination.

We received another call from a contractor working on the highway who asked if we would consider bringing him on as a subcontractor. Remarkably, he had all the tractors, people, equipment, trucks, and expertise needed to get the job done. Initially, I found him arrogant, and I didn't care for him. Despite this feeling, I bit my tongue, realizing I didn't have to go home with him; we just needed him to do great work. And there's more to the story.

Shortly after, an email came in that would blow our minds! Due to errors in calculating the bid numbers, the $39.99 Lawn Care Guy won the two other bids we had submitted as well. We quickly found subcontractors to take on those contracts, and we were going full steam ahead!

We needed more capital, so we negotiated with another business owner in the industry, and he agreed to finance our payroll. We offered a thirty percent return on each payroll cycle he would cover. We knew it might take sixty to ninety days to get paid after the invoices were submitted. We also understood that paying the subcontractors would be crucial in ensuring that everyone who had gone to bat for us would be protected.

Oh yeah, to have some additional cushion, I decided to ask for microloans from my professional network, and those whom I knew had their own. See, I figured what we were initially asking for was just way more than what anyone wanted to risk, so I brought the barrier down to a reasonable ask. The ask was very simple: $5,000 for a sixty-day thirty percent return and a signed promissory note that I generated. Just as planned, I had takers, and just to be sure I did not default or disappoint, I had saved a little cash that was a rainy day fund, which I used to back their funds with each of their names on it.

The first year of the contract went so smoothly; we could not have dreamt it any better. We paid off the tractors in less than six months and gave the owners a nice gift as a thank you, as well as made good on the microloans just as I had promised. There was an exception with the microloans in that one of the givers allowed me to extend for an extra 10% return, so we didn't find ourselves in a cash-poor position. We did lose a couple of contractors and had to replace them, which ended up not being the worst thing because the new guys fitted what we were doing better.

Then, the work was not up to par with the standards of the contract, and it was no walk in the park to get it under control and acceptable to the inspectors. Sometimes you must be willing to lose in the short term to win in the long term. Once we did all the heavy lifting, each subsequent cycle would be easier, thus creating a higher level of profit and ease of work. The only hiccup was the decision to abandon the two other contracts. I supported this decision since the subcontractors had gotten very far behind, and we did not want that to affect other areas. This painful decision would prove to be a very wise one. We pulled the plug and lost a great deal of short-term and long-term money by doing so, but it was worth it.

Year two turned out to be just as smooth as the first one with a few major changes implemented. We decided to remove the burden of direct employment and pay a little extra money to have a long-term employment agency handle all our hiring needs. We figured this would eliminate payroll issues and potential for fraud with handwritten paychecks. This would also remove us from relational issues with employees whom we had known for many years and the favoritism that may disrupt great working environments.

If someone contacted us for hire, we would send them directly to the agency to fill out paperwork and be interviewed. We submitted the exact criteria we were looking for in the various positions we needed, and the agency did an outstanding job of sifting through the many applicants to send us the right candidates. The beauty of it all is it limited a great deal of liability for us while benefiting the agency and its growth in the marketplace. Systems had been created to do the daily tasks of reporting and ensuring each area of the contract was completed with a spirit of excellence, which ironically used to be the phrase printed on the back of the t-shirts of one of the subs.

Within two years, my friend, mentor, brother, and now business partner, the $39.99 Lawn Care Guy, was back. The past stumbles seemed like a distant thought. He decided not to pursue other opportunities and simply concentrate on the one contract that was operating at a high level. My mission was not complete; yet I was in a place where I knew it was time for me to put a little more concentration into building Pro Cutters Lawnscapes, Inc. To be clear, I never saw the two as competitors, and, in my mind, I was 100% on board with our partner administering the contract with me managing the day-to-day operation as I had been doing. My loyalty and commitment could not be questioned, nor would I waiver from the word I gave to God or pledged to him.

Chapter Eleven

THE NEXT CORNER

Pro Cutters Lawnscapes

I gradually regained my momentum, setting up small initiatives for what I anticipated as a significant opportunity ahead. We transformed my wife/business partner's office into a conference room, providing an environment conducive to growth. Being someone who thinks outside the box and embraces innovation, I began inviting people for casual discussions and brainstorming sessions.

If you believe success will leap out at you, keep waiting; you might be there a long time. Success isn't sneaky. Avoid taking the path of least resistance. Resist fear. Resist laziness. Resist quitting. Resist sideline gazing. Resist complacency. Resist jealousy. Resist hate—now, add anything I missed. With all that aside, prepare for your breakthrough!

I realigned myself with who I knew I was destined to be in business, and things were gaining momentum. Predating my reconnection with my partner, I saw a bid while scouring the website for contract opportunities. The bid covered forty-plus properties, varying from 5 to over 40 acres and requiring weekly maintenance. Little did I know, we needed to navigate through three levels to secure the right to submit a bid.

I never envisioned myself as an administrator; but recognizing the need for our growth, I understood the necessity of stepping out of my comfort zone. After submitting the required information, we were elated to receive notice that we were deemed a qualified contractor, which allowed us to proceed to the next level of bid submission.

I was in a zone and, for a moment, didn't consider that we were just submitting a bid. I truly believed we were going to be awarded some of the work. I met with the contract inspectors, administrator, and three other contractors. I can't deny that the properties were huge and in bad shape. For a second, I wondered if they had ever been maintained. Yet, I knew they had been neglected due to a lack of funding with the economy downturn.

I visited all the properties to develop strategies that would help us focus on regional areas requiring a full crew of four to five employees. I spent an entire day at each location. Some sites could be doubled in one trip but would require an additional two crew members. We also would need to invest in new trucks to avoid breakdowns. The furthest property from our headquarters was over two and a half hours one way.

Yeah, I know that's a lot of windshield time. Keep in mind we decided to bid on every property but would submit higher bids for the outliers that were over four hours away. If we won them, we would figure it out at that time. I did my due diligence and broke down the numbers until I believed we would be in a good place if we won several of them and finally submitted our bid. Of course, the whole process took over sixty days to complete. I checked my messages and emails daily to see if we had received a call.

Grass Clips

When you believe wholeheartedly in something, you take on a posture of expectation.

One day, that anticipated call came through with some very good, but surprising news. While I believed we would get some of the work, we had possibly landed more than half of it throughout the state. The representative peppered me with questions, asking if we could handle so many properties that far away and if we had the staff to get it done as specified in the contract. As with most contracts, there could be a 60, 90, or even 120-day wait period for payment, so the company would need to be financially strong enough to float that cost. There was also a huge initial investment necessary to get started, and I knew I better be right with my response and our ability to get the work done before answering. Without blinking, I responded, "We absolutely can take on the work, and they would be glad that we did accept." Talk about having confidence—I lacked none in that department and knew we had completed large contracts before. It would be like riding a bike; once you learn, you never forget. We had been putting away resources financially for over a year, anticipating an opportunity just like this, and now it was here.

Necessary Changes

In years prior, as we were growing the business, I concentrated on being different and standing out, which worked for that vision. As I pondered where we were at this juncture, I knew things would need to be modified, and a new vision would emerge. We decided that the color scheme of our trucks and uniforms should be changed. We just needed to keep it simple. We also decided to change out all our box trucks and not paint them any color; we would buy them in white.

Even though I was feeling reinvigorated, the darkness of the building we were leasing loomed heavily over me, and I knew we would need a fresh start in that department as well. I began looking for buildings until one day a thought ran across my mind that maybe we just need to build what we wanted and secure some land. This was a huge step as we were operating under an oath of debt-free living for not only our personal lives but for the business as well. Searching daily, I found a two-point-four-acre plot less than five miles from where we were located at the time. Immediately when I went to look at the land, I knew this would be the place for our growth and pitched the idea to my trusted business partner and wife, and we agreed to move forward.

Since she was a real estate agent also, the process was very simple. We quickly got the land under contract. After doing some research, I found a commercial truck dealership and sent an email to a salesperson listed on their site, telling him exactly what we were looking for in a box truck. Things were falling right into place. The company we used to survey the land was also able to give us a drawing of the building we envisioned that could be sent to the city for approval.

As we awaited the response, we continued planning our exit from the building we had occupied for the last ten years. I contacted our landlord, informing him of our contemplation to relocate and inquiring about the penalty for breaking our lease. Despite his disappointment with our potential departure, he agreed to let us stay on a month-to-month basis until we were ready to leave, without imposing any penalties. Moreover, he extended an offer for us to purchase the building, along with the adjacent one, at a very favorable price.

Considering what I know today, we should have given it more thought, as it would have been a lucrative investment. At the time, it didn't align with our growth strategy. Unaware of the time it would take to construct our new headquarters, the city's response turned out to be a blessing in disguise. The message essentially conveyed, "You can't build a simple warehouse; here are the new specs for approval." This caught us off guard, realizing we couldn't afford the proposed building modifications, which would significantly escalate the costs.

While standing on the land, I recalled one of the owners from the survey company expressing a wish to have known us before we bought the land. Intrigued, I inquired why, and he mentioned having a building that he believed would suit our needs. Engaging in due diligence, we examined approximately five buildings in the area, but none aligned with our vision for the business's future.

We reconvened with the surveyor at the land to discuss his findings from soil samples and the process of digging holes to assess the amount of rock on the property. The results revealed a significant presence of rock, indicating the need for blasting when construction commenced. Overwhelmed, I felt the urge to take a walk to clear my head. As we concluded the meeting with the surveyor, he once again mentioned the building he owned. Both our business manager and I exchanged glances before asking about its location. To our surprise, he mentioned it was right down the street, within walking distance of the land we had purchased, and he offered to show it to us.

Networking Opportunities

With everything aligning seamlessly, I recognized the importance of not becoming complacent with my dreams and aspirations if I wanted to elevate the business to greater heights. The large corporation we had pitched to a few years prior remained a top priority, and I delved into strategic planning to establish a relationship with them. One of the initial steps was to join an organization for minority businesses in metro Atlanta, even though I wasn't optimistic about opportunities solely based on my ethnicity.

My perspective shifted slightly after a conversation with a close friend who encouraged me to see it differently. It became an opportunity to forge relationships that might otherwise be elusive. Embracing this perspective, we completed the extensive paperwork required for certification as an MBE *(Minority Business Enterprise)*. I've never been one to beg or join groups solely for personal gain, so, as with all networking groups, my approach was to cultivate genuine connections by offering encouragement and assistance to others.

We started attending numerous events, aiming to connect with individuals and understand more about the organization and the corporations supporting it. Despite having specific targets for future business endeavors, we chose to maintain an open mind, allowing potential opportunities to unfold organically.

The MBE organizes an annual event known as *The Business Opportunity Expo*. The objective is to facilitate one-on-one meetings between companies and corporations seeking to engage with MBEs, particularly those gaining traction. I participated in multiple one-on-one sessions, enthusiastically presenting our company. I conveyed our identity and elaborated on our future aspirations. While I felt positive about the interactions, I also recognized that such events often serve more for appearances and may not necessarily lead to tangible outcomes.

In my mind, each time a new person or entity became aware of who we were, I made sure they wouldn't forget me, the company, or the presentation. Walking around the event and stopping at various tables highlighting businesses throughout the Southeast Region, I was approached for an impromptu sit-down with a buyer from the corporation with which we wanted to work with. Elated, I immediately accepted the offer and was introduced to the decision-maker. I thought to myself, this is going to be a done deal because all I needed was the chance to shoot my shot, and I wouldn't miss. Let's just say, I shot my shot, and right before it went in, someone moved the basket, and it fell flat, sounding like a thud.

The person I met with seemed uninterested in anything I was saying, and to be brutally honest, was very cold towards me. That is never a good sign. I smiled and was courteous the entire time, not letting my discomfort show, but I knew my meeting was going nowhere. I thanked the person for taking the time to meet with me, and claimed she would be in touch. As it left her mouth to my ears, I knew 100% it was just a courtesy statement, and we would not hear from her.

I walked away shaking my head and wondering what in the world had just happened! For a few seconds, I walked aimlessly around, trying to get my bearings and pick my ego off the floor from the disappointing meeting I had just attended. Then, across the event, someone motioned to me to come to them. It was the contact that had hooked me up for the sit-down with the decision-maker. We sat down, and I was asked how the meeting went, of course, I had to let her know I did not think it went well, and to my surprise, she simply said no worries.

I looked up, and she explained, "You just need to find another way of entry." Our meeting ended, and I stood up, shook off the bad meeting, and prepared to meet some more people. While walking around, I was stopped again by someone in the BOE. She asked if I heard of the Georgia Mentor Protégé Program. I had never heard of it, and they began to explain what it was and what was required to get into the program. I was excited after hearing that they would select over thirty top corporations and over fifty MBEs. The MBEs would then present to these corporations an opportunity to gain a one-year mentorship with their business.

Sounds great, right? Indeed, it did until they told me one of the requirements: you had to be making at least 1 million dollars a year in revenue. Unfortunately, for us, we had not reached that point with Pro Cutters Lawnscapes, Inc., and had no idea when we would. I responded to the representative, explaining our status and that we would not qualify for the opportunity. They said they understood and encouraged us to pursue it anyway, as we never know what may happen. I decided to bet on our future.

After days of contemplation, we decided to apply for the opportunity. We were initially told we didn't qualify, but a few days later, we received another notice allowing us to present anyway. Let's pause for a moment… If you've felt doubted, counted out, or considered giving up, stand tall, find a mirror, and affirm, "I have everything necessary to succeed. I will not give up or give in. I am prepared and ready." Then, go do what you know you need to do!

The Surveyor's Property

We approached the building for a walk-around, and immediately, I thought to myself, "I don't think this will work for us." The building we currently leased was on one level, featuring a large roll-up door allowing us to park trucks inside and secure equipment. The prospective place was split-level, with no provision for parking vehicles inside the basement area.

The upper level housed seven offices and two conference rooms, while the lower section had an open bay, one office, and fenced-in exterior parking.

Our business manager and I asked for a few minutes to discuss and explore further, to which he agreed, encouraging us to take our time. As he exited, I shared my concerns with our business manager about lacking immediate access to downstairs due to steps. He nodded, suggesting I needed to envision it based on what was to come rather than where we were at that moment. It's worth noting that we had no other managers at the time, except for myself, so I would be the sole person in the building regularly. I closed my eyes and pictured the growth we expected to have one day. Shortly after, I realized he was right.

Grass Clips

Keep an open mind to those whom God has placed around you. Their insights and opinions may differ from yours, but they might align with what God desires for you.

To not sound too needy, we expressed our gratitude to the owner and mentioned that we would get back to him soon if we found the building suitable for our needs. Although initially, my trusted business partner and wife didn't see the potential, she, in the spirit of trusting my opinion and leadership, yielded. Together, we began mapping out how everything would work. Part of the dilemma was the uncertainty around purchasing the land and not proceeding as expected. It made me question whether I had heard God correctly, but His voice seemed certain, and we just needed to pause.

We met with the owners of the building, learned about its history and the reasons for selling and began negotiations. Then, a significant hurdle arose immediately: we were adamant about not using credit or signing a traditional lease. While buying the building outright was not feasible now, we were equally unwilling to rent again. You might be wondering how we planned to build a new facility with limited cash flow and no financing, and your question is valid. Frankly, I had no clear plan and anticipated addressing that challenge when the time came. Faith doesn't always provide immediate answers to every question as to our liking, but it does assure us that, in time, nothing will go unanswered according to His plan!

I pondered and pondered some more, attempting to devise a proposal that made sense and, hopefully, would be acceptable. After much prayer, I decided to present a bold proposition to them. I suggested a substantial upfront payment to the owners, framing it as a down payment for a lease-to-own arrangement with a few variations. One option involved a one year lease, with the intention to purchase the building after the year concluded.

All payments exceeding their exact mortgage payment would contribute to paying down the note on the property. I reasoned that by consistently paying extra each month with any overflow, the final payment to purchase the building wouldn't feel burdensome. When I gave them the substantial initial pay-ment and assured them that, in the event of default, they could keep the initial amount, and we would vacate the premises with no strings attached, they exchanged glances and asked, "Are you sure?"

Confidence radiated from every fiber of my being at this point, and I introduced a slight curveball: "Let's add a clause: if for some reason we can't close the transaction in one year, we will extend for an additional year and cover their taxes and the insurance for that period." They nodded in agreement, and the deal was all but sealed. They would provide the paper-work, and we would submit a cashier's check for the substantial down payment, and just like that, we secured our next business location—boldly named headquarters.

Standing on the steps leading to the outside area, I peered beyond the borders of the property and nonchalantly asked, "Who owns the property behind this one?" They did not know. This prompted me to suggest they find out and determine the extent of their land ownership. In my mind, I was envisioning expansions, even though the space currently had more land than we needed. I understood that, in planning, it would be wise to not plan for where we currently were but to plan for the destination God has shown us.

We signed the contract and had sixty days to move in because a tenant was occupying the basement area, and we didn't want to immediately displace him. We were elated, and I decided not to share the good news with anyone outside of my immediate prayer circle. This allowed us to walk the prop-erty in prayer, and I could strategize our exit from the current property. Several weeks later, the owners of the new property informed us that they tracked down the owner of the property behind us. We asked if they were interested in selling an acre behind us for future expansion.

They inquired, and the person was willing to sell. Without any hesitation, we purchased the land outright and would sit on it until the appropriate time. To avoid any misunderstanding, the land was 100% useless without the other acres they owned or the building we were moving into. You might wonder why we bought land connected to a property we did not own and what we would do if the deal fell through. My answer is that I did not entertain thoughts of what could go wrong, only thoughts of what would certainly come to us in the future. There was never an ounce of doubt!

We entered the third year of the partnership with the $39.99 Lawn Care Guy, and everything was going exceptionally well. No complaints surfaced about the contracted work, and everyone involved with the various teams was content and thriving. As we geared up for a move, I called a meeting to announce the change. That Friday marked the day we would relocate all our assets to a new building permanently. The moment was bittersweet as I sensed the timing was right, and we were leaving behind the occasional dark cloud that seemed to hover over us.

The Georgia Mentee Protégé Program

In the interim between agreeing to the terms of the new building and our impending move, we received an invitation to present our company for a spot in a year-long mentorship program. With just five to seven minutes to make our case, we needed to convey why we would be an ideal candidate for a highly successful corporation to invest a year in mentoring our business for growth. I always strive to deliver unique presentations, aiming to leave a lasting impression that they won't soon forget.

The presentations began at 8:30 a.m., showcasing over forty potential MBEs. By sheer luck, we were selected to go next to last. In my mind, I anticipated that everyone would be tired, and my words might resonate like Charlie Brown's teacher—wooont, wooont, wooont—leaving them checked out. When my turn arrived, I discarded the traditional presentation approach, opting for something designed to captivate and grab their attention.

So, I asked everyone to stand up, acknowledging that it had been a long day filled with numerous high-performing MBEs, each deserving of an opportunity. Politely, I urged them to shake off their tiredness and get rejuvenated. I requested some space for the exercise to ensure participants wouldn't bump into the person beside them. I led them through an old Army exercise we called "Kill the Fly." Each person would stretch their arms out, making small circles forward. Upon my command, they'd stop and "kill the fly" *(clap their hands)*, followed by bigger circles and reversing directions, clapping after each completion. I then instructed them to keep "killing the fly," creating a loud applause in unison. Encouraging them to clap faster, the applause grew until it echoed on the street. Like Moses at the Red Sea, I lifted my hands for them to stop, stating that I always wanted a standing ovation before I presented. Laughter erupted, and as they took their seats, I knew I had made a memorable impression!

As everyone settled in, I commenced my pitch with: "If you're seeking a company with all the experience to join your team, we won't be a good fit. If you want a company with all the answers, we shouldn't be considered. If you desire a company that never messes up, we certainly won't be a good match for you. If you want a company that is eager to learn, that will go the extra mile, that will represent you well in the marketplace, then Pro Cutters Lawnscapes, Inc. is the company that will be a match for you." I shared a bit of information about us and concluded by thanking them for the opportunity. Several weeks later, we received notice that the company to whom we gave that PowerPoint presentation decided to mentor us, and we had several other companies inquiring as well!

We stepped into a new phase of business legitimization, and the commitment of a major company to mentor us was the cherry on top. Recalling the dreams of my younger self walking up to corporate headquarters with a briefcase brought a smile to my face, underscoring my appreciation for the journey we had traversed. In our inaugural meeting, we met our mentor and identified three pivotal areas that we believed would propel us to the next level. Given my thorough research on the company, I understood several facets that held immense importance for them.

While our primary goal was growth, we were equally determined to align with their core values. Safety emerged as the foremost priority, serving as the cornerstone of our mentorship. It was closely followed by priorities in financial stability and scalability. The focus on financial stability revolved around ensuring our books were in impeccable order and devising strategies for growth, sans the pursuit of external financing. This decision resonated with our steadfast commitment to realizing our dreams without resorting to conventional funding routes.

I requested their safety manual to study and improve our safety protocols and handbook. Initially, we didn't delve into discussions about working together. Instead, I aimed to concentrate on extracting the assistance that could enhance our appeal for future opportunities. Joint sessions with all the other participants and their mentors every other month were a significant aspect of the program that made a real difference.

Surrounded by rapid scaling, top-notch companies during the mentoring sessions, the landscaping business we owned felt like it was in a league of its own. The question lingered: had we truly arrived? These gatherings not only required updates on our progress in key areas agreed upon with the mentoring companies but also provided invaluable insights from our high-performing peers. This shared experience motivated Shawn and me to navigate the challenges and maximize the opportunity presented. Attending the sessions together added to the gratification of the journey.

Then it happened: the CEO of a construction company stood up to deliver her report on goals and growth strategies, mentioning their pursuit of a thirty-million-dollar five-year opportunity. Immediately, I took note and whispered to myself, "You are dreaming too small, Steve!" A surge of excitement and anticipation washed over me. Witnessing someone in our group thinking on such a grand scale ignited a fire within me. My determination and gratitude surged.

Even to this day, we remain profoundly grateful to our mentor company for taking a chance on a small landscaping business with big dreams and imparting the crucial knowledge necessary for sustained growth. Beyond the knowledge, they bestowed upon us a sense of belonging and exposed us to the corporate realm, providing a substantial level of legitimacy. Despite my inherent confidence, I acknowledge the importance of humility, leaving space for others to contribute to our journey.

The pinnacle of our participation in the program, or so I believed, occurred during a weekend at Callaway Gardens. The event featured multiple classes and an Expo, providing each company with a platform to showcase their products and services. This opportunity allowed potential buyers and corporations to gain insights into what we could offer, fostering mutual growth in the process.

As a visual thinker, I always strive to bring creativity to presentations. To achieve this, I ensured a sharp and professional attire for every meeting. Additionally, I aimed for a distinctive giveaway, a memorable catchphrase, and crystal-clear communication about our services, preempting questions with well-prepared answers. We met with an architect through a contact to bring my visual presentation idea to life. Using a PowerPoint presentation featuring images of our work on a loop. The rendering we created showcased our unique services, emphasizing our capacity for growth and how our skills could contribute to potential partnerships.

Our display included a highway and rest area, highlighting two key areas of focus: highway mowing and commercial landscape maintenance. We depicted tractors being transported on a model tractor trailer and a simulated grass-mowing scenario on a sloped area off the highway. In the rest area, we used scaled commercial lawnmowers to illustrate the nature of our services. Safety cones adorned with "Safety First" labels were strategically placed near vehicles, tractors, mowers, and pedestrian entry points. The model featured elements like grass, trees, shrubs, buildings, and equipment, emphasizing our ability to think innovatively.

On the display board, we prominently featured our core values, company name, logo, and our slogan, "All You Need is Grass... We'll Take Care of The Rest!" After each presentation, I often added, "And if you don't have grass, we can bring that too!"

We also distributed small hand sanitizer samplers with the slogan, "Keep your hands clean and let us do the dirty work!" I must admit, I felt a bit nervous before the presentation, but after engaging with a few visitors, I found my stride, explaining our services like a seasoned veteran. The positive feedback was overwhelming, culminating in the highlight of the awards ceremony where we received the "Best Display in Show" award— ironically, the first award for Pro Cutters Lawnscapes, Inc.

As the event wrapped up, the Georgia Minority Supplier Diversity Council distributed gift bags containing tokens and a book. Surprisingly, we received the wrong bag intended for mentors, and inside was a book titled "Love Works" by Joel Manby. Unaware at the time, this book would significantly impact our journey. Departing that weekend, I was on a high, feeling that our time had indeed arrived.

New Levels

Before leaving our previous business location of ten years, a new tenant introduced himself. Welcoming him, I shared my name, and he expressed interest in looking around, which I happily allowed. He seemed amiable and was considering the building for car repairs. Although our encounter held no immediate significance, as he departed, memories flooded back to the day we first moved into that business space. Back then, we faced uncertainties about covering lease payments, but we fervently prayed to navigate the challenges seamlessly.

Throughout all our challenges, we never once had a late lease payment. A profound sense of gratitude filled my heart as I reflected on God's unwavering faithfulness. At that moment, I called the landlord and informed him that we would cover two months' rent for the new tenant. We left behind furniture and a very clean shop for him. Interestingly, I never directly communicated our gesture to the new tenant. My heart overflowed with fulfillment, and as I walked out of the building for the last time, I didn't glance backward; instead, I eagerly looked forward, excited for the new levels awaiting us in our journey.

Grass Clips

Generosity plants it's seeds, and
there's no need for givers to broadcast each act,
for the seed never forgets where it has been planted.
How you depart one phase of life determines
how you enter the next.

Chapter Twelve

GERMINATION

A Land Called Plentiful

*A*s we settled into our new building; I recognized the need for a crucial step in our growth. I had to develop a management plan for someone who wouldn't be involved in hands-on work but would serve as an administrator and leader. This marked a significant departure from my previous belief that, beyond Shawn's role, others had to contribute physically for us to afford them.

As I observed and absorbed lessons from our mentorship, I understood that my mindset needed a shift for us to reach our full potential. The initial addition to our management team was an individual with highway work experience. Despite facing setbacks in his life, our interactions and his dedication convinced me of his trustworthiness. Trust became a crucial criterion, and humility followed closely behind, recognizing that having reliable team members is a significant barrier to growth for small businesses. He assumed the role of our primary contact for all contracts at that time.

His number became our first point of contact for any task, and we allocated him an office in the downstairs bay. He proved to be precisely what we required, relieving a bit of responsibility from my plate. Every day, I would arrive at the new office between 4 to 5 a.m., ensuring that everyone had the necessary supplies and paperwork for the day with his support as a valuable backup. While I was in my office one day, having spent several months in the new space, it occurred to me how much room we had. I found myself alone in the upstairs area, which featured seven offices, two conference rooms, two bathrooms, a foyer, a receptionist area, and a kitchen. It became evident that we needed another leader. Coincidentally, around that time, my good friend and trusted business manager accepted a position as an assistant principal at a local middle school. I felt genuinely happy for him, as education was not just a job for him but a family tradition and rite of passage—his parents, late sister, and wife had all been educators.

I didn't want to obstruct what I believed to be his calling, so I supported him wholeheartedly, encouraging him to make a difference in the school system. True to form, he went on to initiate an aerospace program at the middle school and continued to impact young men through his non-profit organization, Men of Distinction. Recognizing the need for a person with trustworthiness, strong character, humility, a moral compass, family orientation, and high integrity in the vacant position, I set out to find the right fit.

Without much thought, I had a person in mind, a gentleman from our church who reached out. We chatted about a possible position with the company. See, I had been watching him for about four years, and even though I already knew he was the guy, we went through the process of interviewing anyway, just to be 100% sure. We sent him an application, and he responded with his resume, which I have to say was very impressive, and the process began. On the day of his interview, I glanced at my watch and felt disappointed that he was not on time.

Given what I already knew about him, his tardiness did not align with the character I had come to expect. Therefore, I chose to give him the benefit of the doubt.

About five minutes past the agreed-upon time, I noticed a car pulling up, and it appeared to be him rushing out of the driver's seat, looking somewhat disheveled. His pants were torn down the side of his leg, and he was breathing heavily. I inquired if everything was okay, and he explained that he had been in an accident on the way to the office, where someone hit him. He exchanged information with the other party because he couldn't afford to wait for the police and risk missing his appointment. At that moment, although I felt the formalities were unnecessary, we still went through the interview process to maintain professionalism even though he was already hired in my mind.

We offered him the position of division manager, and just like that, I had the second-in-command on board. One notable aspect of the hiring process was an email he sent me after I mentioned we would get back to him post-interview despite having already made up my mind to hire him. The email expressed his gratitude for the opportunity and concluded with a statement of his willingness to work for thirty days with no pay to demonstrate his value. While I hadn't considered not paying him, I appreciated the gesture and assured him that we would soon find out if his words held.

Over the years, he evolved into a valued and highly trusted executive member of our team, surpassing all expectations I had when entering our partnership. With him on board, we began to take shape into the formidable business I envisioned. We allocated the office next to mine for him, while the other team members working on the highway received offices on the opposite side of the building.

Family Matters

I received a text from an unfamiliar number, as I read it, I realized it was from one of my cousins from South Carolina. He told me he moved to metro Atlanta and needed a job, which immediately made me grimace. I made it a point not to hire or suggest employment to family members since I preferred to keep our relationships strictly familial. Many businesses are family-owned and work well together, while others experience strained relationships when mixing family and business.

I responded to his text and told him to call me, which he immediately did. We caught up on family matters and discussed how everyone was doing. His grandmother and my mother were sisters, and we had a very close-knit family while growing up in the country. Emotions overwhelmed me as I heard echoes of my aunt, uncle, and his mother in his voice. I realized

I could not turn my back on him; I needed to offer whatever assistance we could. He was in a dilemma because he needed a place to stay and, like many young adults including myself at his age, had made some poor choices that hindered him from securing a place.

My business manager and I discussed the best way to assist him. We reached out to some property owners, explaining the situation and inquiring about their willingness to give the young man a chance with our corporate backing. After numerous calls, a gentleman in the next county agreed to rent out a townhome to him. We assured the property owner that the rent would be paid on time each month, with our company backing him. To alleviate any initial stress, we also made the first couple of months' payments upfront.

Before hiring him, I asked him to make a vow not to disclose our relationship and not to seek any special treatment. I made it clear that our company operated without favoritism and treated everyone based on their performance. He agreed to these terms, and we proceeded with the hiring process. As he joined the team, he proved to be an invaluable asset, serving as a trustworthy supervisor on one of the trucks. His passion for landscaping and strong work ethic further contributed to his positive impact on the company's growth.

After a couple of years in our new building, he requested a few days off to visit his children and the rest of the family in South Carolina, which was nothing unusual as he went home often. I told him to enjoy himself and to tell everyone I said hello, not knowing it would be the last time I would see him alive. The next morning, I had a conversation with one of my cousins in Connecticut, and she mentioned that everyone was praying for him and his family.

She had no idea he worked for us. I asked her what she meant, and she replied, "You didn't know? He was stabbed last evening and is in the hospital." Stunned, I made a quick U-turn, headed home to grab a bag, and rushing to the hospital in South Carolina. I called his mother, informing her of my imminent arrival and offering prayers.

I returned home, packed a bag, and informed my wife of the situation. She embraced me, urging caution on the drive and requesting updates. As I set out, not even two miles from home, my phone rang. My cousin's mother was wailing on the other end, delivering the heartbreaking news that he had passed away. Crushed, I returned home in disbelief. On Monday, I gathered the team, revealing that he was murdered over the weekend and that he was my cousin.

The impact was profound, and a lingering somberness enveloped everyone. As a company, we decided to organize a tribute by sending six trucks and approximately twenty-five crew members, including his landscaping team, to South Carolina for the funeral. His picture adorned one of the trucks, driven by his crew in his honor. This special truck led the funeral procession from his mother's house to the church of my childhood. The display of love and appreciation, along with a large portrait showcasing his various work sites and a client's heartfelt email commending his exceptional work, left his mother, sisters, and the entire family deeply moved.

The funeral took an unexpected turn as our division manager, and I was asked to speak on his behalf. As I stood up to address the gathering, the entire team, impeccably dressed in uniform, rose, and stood tall. They remained standing until I concluded my remarks and returned to my seat. On that day, we moved as one to honor our fallen brother, and I couldn't have been prouder of a company having team members who genuinely cared for each other.

Grass Clips

Never stop treating your team with respect and appreciation.

Our First Commercial Property

After a year in our new building, we opted to extend our lease, allowing an additional year to secure ownership. Even though we had the means to purchase outright, it would strain our cash flow.

Throughout the year, diligent extra payments brought us closer to a manageable closing price. We also honored our commitment by covering our landlord's taxes and insurance.

As the business thrived, we grew steadily. Before year-end, I informed the landlord of our readiness to finalize the purchase. On closing day, I approached with focus, ready to own our first commercial building—a significant step forward. Entering the attorney's office, pleasantries gave way to the business at hand.

At the closing, we received a binder with the necessary documents, and as anyone familiar with such proceedings knows, there's a considerable amount of signing involved. Everything appeared in order, but as we neared the end, the closing attorney inquired about our financing arrangements. Momentarily caught off guard, I confidently responded, "Ah, yes, that would be with the Bank of Bromell." I then offered a slight smile, reaching into my blazer pocket to produce a cashier's check for the building's balance, while handing it over.

With the acquisition of our first brick-and-mortar building, Pro Cutters Lawnscapes, Inc. achieved a significant milestone. Although Shawn and I celebrated this achievement, I chose not to broadcast it widely, recognizing it as a positive step in the right direction but still just one step on our journey. Over the next few years, our focus remained on continued growth, expanding our management team, and positioning the company for further success.

An opportunity arose for us to be considered for an annual business excellence award, recognizing contributions to the community. The awards were categorized by supplier size, and we found ourselves in the supplier two categories, revenues from one million to ten million. Yes, we had finally hit the seven figure earnings mark. After thorough deliberation and with our mentor company sponsoring us, we decided to proceed with the application process. Crafting a compelling company narrative and compiling extensive data became a rigorous undertaking. We invested significant time in highlighting key areas that set us apart, positioning us competitively against other nominees.

The awards ceremony, a black tie event attended by thousands, promised the announcement of winners in various categories. It was held in a splendid venue in downtown Atlanta, and the anticipation surrounding the event was palpable.

The Annual Award

The much-anticipated night arrived, and we sat with our sponsors and mentors, filled with anticipation. I would be dishonest if I claimed we were extremely confident about the results, given that we were in the lower revenue bracket for the Class II Supplier of the Year Award. It marked our inaugural venture into a prestigious award opportunity. Winning in our category meant qualifying for a regional award, and success there could elevate us to the Supplier of the Year for the entire United States—an almost year-long process.

As we perused the impressive booklet showcasing each competing company in our category, the reality of being among seven others vying for the Class II Supplier of the Year in our affiliate organization sank in. Following the presentation of other corporate awards and lifetime achievements, the time arrived for the Supplier of the Year announcements. Starting with Supplier I, the announcements proceeded in order.

While seated, I grappled with a mix of confidence and doubt. Thoughts crossed my mind about the perception of our business—just a company that cuts grass. I pushed away those thoughts, quickly reminding myself that we were more than a grass-cutting business; we built a formidable enterprise doing business the right way, using lawn care as the avenue to showcase our commitment to excellence in business ownership.

As the announcer listed our names among the nominees, there was a moment of suspense when they pulled out an envelope. Then, with a pause, they declared, "...and the winner for Class II Supplier of the Year is Pro Cutters Lawnscapes, Inc."

At that moment, my eyes sought out my beautiful wife and business partner, Shawn. Rising to my feet, I gave her a wink, pulled out her chair, and reached for her hand. While part of me wanted to shout, "YES! YES! YES!" I composed my emotions. With the audience's enthusiastic applause, we walked hand in hand to the podium to accept the GMSDC Class II Supplier of The Year Award.

We secured the award, posed for photos, and participated in an interview in their green room. Congratulations poured in, and we were on cloud nine. Let me pause for a moment to emphasize that I stopped in my tracks and gave God the credit for all He had allowed us to accomplish up until that point. I thanked Him for what He would continue to do for us in the future.

Grass Clips

*Never let significant victories inflate your ego
to the point where they lead to a
more substantial downfall.*

We shared photos of the evening with our supporters and family, expressing our gratitude and captioning it "We did it!!" I must admit that I hesitated to inform anyone about attending the event because I wanted to avoid disappointment just in case we didn't win. However, business success should never hinge on a single event, whether positive or negative. True success is an accumulation of numerous small victories that grow into significant ones, along with some setbacks. Losses strengthen your business acumen and determination, enabling you to persevere in environments that may have initially seemed unattainable and unwelcoming.

Chapter Thirteen

KEEP GOING, KEEP GROWING

Waves of Success

iding the wave of success, we approached the fifth
year of the contract we managed with the $39.99
Lawn Care Guy, and the looming rebidding process presented a challenge with the added necessity of being
bonded. The bid package was issued in proposal form covering
various areas in the state, requiring us to make some strategic
decisions. After thorough discussions, it became evident that
we would step up, and the other company would submit a proposal independently. Initially, I had no intention of taking this
route, being content with continuing our representation of the
current company.

I decided to steer our company towards other sectors, such
as utility firms, landscape maintenance, vegetation removal,
and municipality right-of-way, and felt content with our current

position. After submitting the proposals, the results showed that only four out of the six companies were deemed qualified and responsive, advancing to the next round. The subsequent steps would be contingent on the pricing for the work, prompting us to embark on a rigorous number-crunching process. While not insurmountable given our experience as a subcontractor, it would certainly pose its challenges.

Simultaneously, as we were engrossed in the bid process and anticipating the outcomes, we received a call to progress to the next round of the NMSDC Supplier of The Year. This phase involved a downtown meeting to review our initial submissions and gain insights on how to enhance our information for the final round. Despite contemplating holding back due to our ongoing substantial growth and numerous concurrent activities, we decided to press on.

We forged ahead and implemented some changes to our application. At this point, our revenue had surged, and our growth trajectory was steep. We invested extensive hours in rewriting and carefully selecting images for our projects, aiming to give us a competitive advantage or at least a fighting chance. A crucial focus was our community engagement and our commitment to uplifting others, including our team members. As the deadline loomed, our business manager, my wife, and I collaborated to finalize the submission. With both the major bid and the Supplier of The Year submission underway, all we could do was wait anxiously.

The Lost Bid

Sitting at my desk, scrolling through the website to check for any highway mowing awards, I prepared myself for what I anticipated to be a moment of relief and celebration. As I scanned the bid awards, my heart sank past my feet. At the top, the apparent low bidder or winner was listed, and a few lines below, our name appeared among the "not low bid" or "no bid submitted" list. To my disbelief, another company initially deemed unqualified secured the apparent win.

My mind raced with questions and disbelief. How could a disqualified company submit and win a bid? Moreover, there was no notification to the qualified bidders about this change. Adding insult to injury, the $39.99 Lawn Care Guy didn't submit a bid, and only one other company provided pricing, ultimately winning several bids, including the remaining ones after an initially awarded company declined.

Still working on the current contract, I reassured myself that this was just a simple error that would be promptly corrected, taking several deep breaths to calm down. Yet, a couple of days later, my worst fears materialized—they intended to proceed with the award. Numb and thoroughly confused, I realized this wasn't a situation to accept and move on.

Seeking guidance, I contacted a friend the same one I had invited to the business conference a few years prior who was a top-notch lawyer. He immediately saw a strong case and advised against letting it slide. Typically, in the bidding process, there's a specific window for protests from other bidders after an award is made. Crafting our first letter, we requested all bid tabulations and documents from the entity that solicited the bids. After reviewing the proposals, we submitted our letter, now left to wait for their response.

While awaiting a response, my friend connected us with another lawyer specializing in cases like the one we believed we had, given that our initial lawyer didn't specialize in contract law. After a phone consultation, we scheduled an in-person meeting to retain him as our attorney for the action I hoped we wouldn't have to take.

You might be wondering why we felt wronged; allow me to elaborate. As mentioned earlier, entering the highway mowing industry was challenging for us, with the only entry point being through a subcontracting opportunity. The company awarded the contract had never—truly never—mowed any grass, not even small jobs. This raised questions about how they could pass the proposal process. Each scorecard used by those reviewing bid packages gave them an exceptionally low score, with comments suggesting they shouldn't be allowed to bid on the project. It wasn't just one or two opinions; every reviewer shared the same sentiment. How did they overcome these unanimous assessments?

They protested their initial disqualification and were allowed to resubmit their proposal with a few changes. This time, they hired someone with previous highway mowing experience many years before the bid to act as their manager. You might think they now had the necessary experience, but as per the contract language, an individual's experience is deemed irrelevant if the company itself hasn't personally performed the work. We had attempted a similar approach in the past, facing rejection multiple times, and this criterion was explicitly outlined in the contract language. Despite recommendations against allowing them to bid, they were granted permission after some calls and a closed-door meeting.

To avoid the appearance of an anomaly or preferential treatment, they also permitted another initially disqualified company to bid. The situation unfolded rapidly, and as our current contract was concluding, we had no favorable resolution for the next one. Despite numerous letters and calls, the contract was awarded to a contractor with no prior experience in the most hazardous area in the state. I empathized even more with the company that had the contract before us, although our circumstances were distinctively different.

Despite these facts, they seemed determined to move forward, leaving us no choice but to explore all our options, including what I believed would be the nuclear option—suing them. It was a risky move, and I assumed that once we took it, our chances of working for that entity again would be toast. We were willing to take that risk, given the egregious nature of the situation and the blatant disregard for the processes they had established to govern contract bidding. I tried not to let my emotions take over, aiming to think objectively and make the right decisions, considering the potential far-reaching consequences and unknowns.

As everything unfolded, the company that won the bid reached out to many contractors I knew, asking them to join their team and submit pricing for the work. My phone, along with several associates', including the $39.99 Lawn Care Guy, was ringing off the hook with questions about emails from the owner of the awarded company. Interestingly, he never personally reached out to me. Truth be told, even if he had, I couldn't have brought myself and Pro Cutters to join forces with his company. Instead, I was willing to assist one of our partners who had an opportunity to work as a third-tier subcontractor and handle all the work on rural roads.

After several meetings, the second-tier contractor decided not to move forward, thereby ending any opportunity to work with the new company. I recognized that once the contract was signed and work began, it would essentially be a done deal, and we would have to wait another five years for it to come back around again. It was a challenging time, and while I wasn't thrilled with the situation, I tried to keep my head up, be thankful for what we did have, and look forward to what lay around the next corner for us. Fortunately, our strategic efforts in building relationships in other areas over the years paid off, and I was grateful for the foresight and discernment we had exercised.

Grass Clips

*Regardless of your expectations,
it's crucial never to dismiss the small voice that
speaks to you in challenging times. Allowing bitterness
and spite to take hold never leads to achieving your
desired outcomes; instead, it widens the gap of regret,
weakens your character, and prolongs your misery.*

Our attorney, an incredibly effective albeit expensive one, called to inform me that our lawsuit was prepared, expressing confidence in its high chance of success. Grateful for his efforts in sending multiple letters and preparing the lawsuit, I informed him that we would not be proceeding with legal action. Despite his apparent displeasure, he inquired about the reason behind this decision after taking several deep breaths.

I responded with a question, "Have you ever felt a divine prompting?" He replied, "Steve, say no more." He understood. I assured him he would receive his full fee, as if we had pursued the legal process, and we would consider him for future needs. In that moment, we closed the chapter, choosing to focus on advancing our brand as we had been doing. We completed the contract with excellence, expressing gratitude to the inspectors and administration, and offering our assistance for any future needs.

Even though feeling heartbroken, disappointed, disgusted, regretful, bewildered, and utterly speechless—experiencing a multitude of emotions and more—I found a significant difference this time. Unlike a few years ago when we lost an employee due to a tragic accident and consequently lost a major contract, this time we had done everything the correct way, and we had nothing to do with the results of the moment. I did not wallow in what had been decided and jumped back into the office with a resolve that can only be described as insane confidence in the growth to come.

My determination surged stronger than ever, with no room for thoughts of failure. I dove into exploring new possibilities and discovering avenues for growth. The state mandated vegetation removal to reclaim the right-of-way across its entire highway systems. Swiftly, we crafted a proposal, submitted it, and, within a month, obtained qualification, earning a place on the bidder's list for upcoming solicitations. Soon after, we secured victories in multiple solicitations, successfully executing them by leveraging a subcontractor model.

We ventured into bidding for a new scope of work, focusing on the interstate entry points recognized by the state as crucial for welcoming the traveling public. Our submissions for these areas proved successful, securing several awards that complemented the numerous parcels we were already maintaining near these strategic locations.

Grass Clips

Entrepreneurial success often lies in the ability to pivot gracefully. Embrace change as a powerful ally, not a foe.

The NMSDC Regional Supplier of The Year Award

Upon receiving notification that we didn't secure the NMSDC Regional Supplier of the Year, I instinctively questioned the outcome. Consulting our mentor for clarification on the process, she outlined the expected timeline for result announcements, indicating that the time frame lapsed. Despite her experience with the process, I couldn't shake the feeling that there might be a mistake. She mentioned the company surpassing us regionally would likely emerge as the national winner.

We shared a good laugh, but I maintained my seriousness, expecting an apology soon. A few days later, a call from New York confirmed the issue with their information. Pro Cutters Lawnscapes, Inc. was indeed chosen to represent the Southeast United States for the prestigious NMSDC Class II Supplier of The Year Award. They assured us they would provide all the necessary details for the black tie event, the culmination of their yearly national convention in Chicago, Illinois for that particular year. Our responsibilities were limited to arranging our flights *(NMSDC covered the costs)*, attending the event, enjoying the weekend, participating in a few interviews, and awaiting the final announcement.

One morning, while seated at my desk, I spontaneously decided to visit Panera Bread for breakfast, carrying one of my trusted notebooks tucked into my vest. Despite our inactivity in highway work at that time, I occasionally wore the vest as a reminder that we would one day resume those activities. During breakfast, an overwhelming sensation prompted me to retrieve the notebook and start jotting down the thoughts that were coming to me from God at that precise moment. I began writing fervently, capturing a dialogue where His words were expressed in statements and questions, and I found myself both writing and responding simultaneously.

After my session, I had the next years of business growth outlined in my notebook and my path ordered. Immediately, I set up a group text with my two trusted brothers and simply sent a message with my routine superlatives, concluding with, "It will happen!!" Every day thereafter, like clockwork, I would send a similar message with the closing words, "It will happen!!"

As spring approached, the new bid-winning company hit the ground running and appeared very professional. I was informed they contracted with a company in the metro area to take care of all the major highways and hired several smaller firms to manage the rural routes. This particular contract expanded, providing even more work than when we were doing it in conjunction with the $39.99 Lawn Care Guy.

They even managed to persuade a few of our supervisors to join them, to help them navigate the challenging terrain. The terrain is no walk in the park, even with all the equipment and personnel on the ground. They were also awaiting delivery of their brand-new tractors and had to use smaller mowers to handle certain areas. While this gave those areas a more manicured look, the highway is a massive undertaking, and using regular commercial mowers could increase completion time by five times or more, depending on the number of units available.

As the information came in, I shut it down to avoid succumbing to disparaging thoughts or wishing for their failure. Whenever I started feeling uneasy, I would simply pray for them and focus on the charge given to me for the company to grow. The good news for us is that we stuck to our commitment to be debt-free, save money, and not fund our dreams through credit and installment accounts. This ensured that, regardless of what happened, we would not be moving backward, stressed, and in a position of weakness.

Grass Clips

*Strategic positioning lays the foundation
for opportunities to flourish even
in challenging times.*

Thanks to the financial cushion we built, we experienced no disruptions and continued our growth, expanding into new areas, including operations in another state. I remained steadfast in my commitment not to let any setback derail our path to building a highly successful business.

Over the following months, reports surfaced indicating challenges in the company's performance. As I traveled along the highways to inspect various job sites across the state, I couldn't help but notice tall grass and accumulating trash. Despite these hurdles, I maintained my hopes for the company's success and safety, trusting that they were actively addressing the situation.

One morning, around 1 a.m., I awoke with a strong sense of purpose and an irresistible urge to drive on the highway, seeking divine guidance. Acting on this inexplicable influence, I immediately called my two most trusted friends and brothers, skipping the usual greetings, and instructed them to meet me at the office by 2:30 a.m. before abruptly ending the call.

Without waiting for their responses, I informed my wife about an emergency at the office. After a brief prayer, she wished me safety. Upon reaching the office, I waited for my friends. When they arrived around 2:15 a.m., I walked out and we got into one of their trucks, and no one questioned why.

Grass Clips

Trust is the bedrock of fruitful relationships,
be it personal or professional.

I entered the back seat and instructed Slim, one of the subcontractors and a trusted friend to drive on the Interstate, intending to pray and agree on every stretch until daybreak. Without a specific outcome in mind, I was simply obeying the inner prompting. Our prayers alternated, and at one point, the Full-Size GMC seemed on the verge of turning over due to our heightened praise. By the time we concluded, I had lost my voice. Returning to headquarters, we exchanged glances, uttering the words, "But God." No need to recap; we simply moved forward with our day, and I continued propelling towards business growth.

It is Happening

Over the months, our division manager and I engaged in numerous conversations, mutually learning and benefiting from each other. He consistently fulfilled his commitment to arrive before me and stay after I left each day. Grateful for his presence, we recognized the need to expand our management team. I shared with him that something extraordinary was on the horizon, destined to leave him astonished and bolster his faith like never before. Though he simply nodded in acknowledgment, I couldn't help but wonder if he thought I was a bit over confident. At times, I even questioned my own experiences, considering the stark reality of the challenges we faced. Yet, amid these reflections, the enduring mantra persisted: "It will happen!" and "It is happening!"

On a bright and sunny day, approximately three months into the mowing season with the new crews in full swing, the office phone rang. It's worth noting that I rarely answered the phone, typically letting the answering service handle it. On this occasion, I happened to be in the hallway, and our division manager was there too when we overheard someone saying, "This is *(insert contract holder name)* and we were wondering if Pro Cutters would be interested in taking over the highway mowing contract immediately. Give us a call as soon as possible." The caller continued to provide several numbers just in case we missed them.

I let out a lion-worthy roar to acknowledge just how good God has been! In the office, we laughed and laughed, and I made calls to my trusted business partner and wife, the $39.99 Lawn Care Guy, and Slim, simply saying, "It has happened!!!!" Despite having lost it once more through unbelievable circumstances, we now had it back again! Hope is intriguing. When you hold onto it, you are never out of the running for a win, even if it is delayed, and even if success eludes you in one, two, three, or four attempts. You can't quit because maybe race number five is your podium moment!

We promptly returned their call to understand their expectations and requirements. When asked about the timeframe we needed to mobilize and bring the highway back to its optimal state, I confidently assured them that within two weeks, we would be operational and ready to deliver the excellence we are known for. Excitedly, I contacted our partners, sharing the fantastic news and gauging their readiness, with each expressing their ability to be prepared within the given time frame. In less than two weeks, we were mobilizing and strategizing once again.

Preparations included ordering new uniforms and safety gear for the team, and meticulous scheduling commenced. To make a positive impression on the procurement entity, whom I fondly dubbed "The Head of State," we organized a meet-and-greet at their headquarters. Seven managers, impeccably attired in khaki pants and black oxford shirts adorned with our company logo, presented themselves as a team ready for business, armed with laptops and a well-thought-out action plan.

Later, I discovered there was skepticism about our ability to perform, but at that moment, their choices were limited. Any doubts about our representation were dispelled after our meeting, and within a month of being on the ground, we converted everyone into believers! I take immense pride in highlighting one achievement. Initially, the contractor reached out to all our partners for assistance, but every single one of them declined, without any influence from me. I even communicated to one partner that I would completely understand if they chose otherwise due to their company's financial needs. Curious, I inquired why they turned down the offer, and they responded that it stemmed from the respect, fair treatment, and timely payments we consistently provided, even during periods when we hadn't received payment ourselves.

Grass Clips

*Doing what is right always provides
support in the battle!*

CONCLUSION

The City of Chicago

*W*ith everything running smoothly, we arrived in Chicago for the National Convention of NMSDC and the award banquet. Choosing not to attend the scheduled events, I spent time in the lobby, engaging in conversations and working until we were prepared to explore the city. While Chicago was familiar to me from previous visits, my trusted business partner and wife were eager to do some sightseeing, particularly on the Magnificent Mile.

The latter part of the day was spent leisurely exploring shops and enjoying ourselves until the next day when the awards ceremony was scheduled. Having received notice of expected interviews in preparation for the grand finale, we eagerly prepared for the occasion. In the green room, we encountered potential awardees in our category and others representing different councils. I must admit that some of the interviews left me in awe of the incredible competition we were up against. After our interview, I had an overwhelming sense that we were not there to leave empty-handed and had just as good a chance as anyone else, despite the stiff competition.

As we prepared for the grand night, my confidence soared, even as a fleeting thought of "At least you made it this far" tried to overtake me. I adjusted my bow tie, casting a glance at my stunningly beautiful wife as she placed her hand on my arm.

Together, we walked into the elegantly decorated ballroom, guided to our reserved table, and enjoyed our dinner. As the event commenced, the moderator announced the highlight of the evening—the NMSDC Supplier of the Year Awards across four categories.

Despite already being briefed on the process, they explained the procedure and steps to take if announced as winners. Knowing that the chances of winning increased after the runner-up was announced, we eagerly awaited the results. The winners for Class I *(revenues of 1 million and under)* were announced, followed by Class II *(annual revenues from 1 million to 10 million)*. Then came the moment of heightened anticipation, and with a deliberate pause, they proclaimed, "And the winner for NMSDC Class II Supplier of The Year is... Pro Cutters Lawnscapes, Inc.!!!"

As Shawn and I exchanged smiles, we walked onto the stage, accepting the award in front of a captivated audience of over a thousand people, all impeccably dressed. After a few words of gratitude, the event concluded, and in the lobby, a young lady approached me. She asked for a moment, and I gladly obliged. Leaning in, she remarked, "You guys must cut a hell of a lot of grass." I chuckled and nodded, affirming, "Yes, we do!"

Reflecting on our humble beginnings as original partners, I recalled the day we ventured into business by assembling a lawnmower from a box on my father's, James O. Homer's, southwest Atlanta lawn. This milestone marked a journey of perseverance, faithfulness, unwavering belief, resilience, and trust in God—a well-earned payoff. Holding the "SOYA" *(Supplier of The Year Award)* that evening, I wished I could convey to my mother in person, "Mommy, despite life's obstacles, your baby boy made it... unfortunately, I could not." Amid a hint of sadness, I smiled, deeply grateful for the enduring journey we had envisioned.

Even Maggots Grow Wings and Escape the Depths of Despair

Contemplating my early years, I reminisce about looking through the space that once housed our bathroom—a void reverberating with the discouraging words of my uncle, who doubted my potential. It dawned on me that in life, we hold the power to turn negativity, harsh words, and the adverse actions of others into catalysts for positive outcomes.

After years of hard work and unwavering belief, the moment of accomplishment finally arrived, allowing me to gaze into the mirror with profound joy. Overwhelmed, I reminded myself not to settle but to dream even bigger. From the little boy navigating the aftermath of a hurricane, to the teenager grappling with a career-altering injury, and then finding my way in the US Army, becoming a young father, establishing a relationship with God, getting married, and overcoming trials in the complex business world for a mere taste of success, here we stood—winners on a national stage.

In the subsequent years, we persevered in building a robust business. Starting with a meager $200 Target card, we evolved into a debt-free enterprise operating across multiple states. Today, we proudly stand as a top 150 Landscape Business in America, surpassing 8 figures in annual revenue. I share these achievements not to boast but to acknowledge the significance of faithfulness and perseverance. Valuable accomplishments often emerge from hardships, tough choices, soul-searching, and the vision to look beyond current challenges toward a brighter future.

Grass Clips

Dream larger and never allow anyone to
convince you that your aspirations are unattainable.
You possess the capabilities required if you believe
and are ready to invest the effort.

On your journey, you'll encounter those destined to sow seeds in your life, others to nurture and water your growth, and some you're meant to inspire and support with your seeds and care. Never underestimate times of failure; they are merely springboards to eventual success in life. As the chapters of your narrative unfold every day, enriched by the gift of life, your odyssey will persist in expanding, constructing, and bestowing blessings upon others.

May this business narrative propel you towards immense success and inspire you to view failure not as the conclusion of your dreams but as a placeholder to remember that "With God, all things are possible."